THY WILL BE DONE

THY WILL BE DONE

E. M. BOUNDS

Whitaker House

Editor's note: This book has been edited for the modern reader. Words, expressions, and sentence structure have been updated for clarity and readability.

THY WILL BE DONE
(Originally titled *The Reality of Prayer*)

ISBN: 0-88368-449-7
Printed in the United States of America
© 2000 by Whitaker House

Whitaker House
30 Hunt Valley Circle
New Kensington, PA 15068

Library of Congress Cataloging-in-Publication Data

Bounds, Edward M. (Edward McKendree), 1835–1913.
      Thy will be done / by E. M. Bounds.
        p.   cm.
      ISBN 0-88368-449-7 (pbk. : alk. paper)
      1. Prayer—Christianity. 2. Jesus Christ—Prayers. I. Title.
  BV210.2.B678 2000
  248.3'2—dc21

                                                  00-008799

    2 3 4 5 6 7 8 9 10 11 12 / 09 08 07 06 05 04 03 02 01

Contents

Introduction

Edward McKendree Bounds was born in north-eastern Missouri on August 15, 1835. As a young man, he practiced law for three years before he felt called to preach the Gospel. He was ordained in the Methodist church in 1859.

He also served as a Confederate chaplain during the Civil War. For a short time, he was held as a prisoner of war in Nashville, Tennessee. After being released, he returned to Franklin, Tennessee, where he and the Confederate troops had suffered a great defeat in battle. He could not forget about the people of Franklin, so he sought out a half dozen men who believed in the power of prayer. For over a year, they met every Tuesday night to pray for revival, and God answered their prayers.

Bounds rose every day at 4 A.M. to pray. The Reverend Claude L. Chilton, musical composer, fellow minister, and a close friend of his, wrote:

> As breathing is a physical reality to us, so prayer was a reality for Bounds. He took the command, *"Pray without ceasing"* (1 Thess. 5:17) almost as literally as nature takes the law that controls our breathing. He did not merely pray well that he

might write well about prayer. He prayed because the needs of the world were upon him. He prayed, for long years, upon subjects that the easygoing Christian rarely gives a thought, and for objects that men of less thought and faith are always ready to call impossible. From his solitary prayer vigils, year by year, there arose teaching equaled by few men in modern Christian history. He wrote transcendently about prayer, because he was himself transcendent in its practice.

Bounds was a man who ever lived on prayer ground. He walked and talked with the Lord. Until his death on August 24, 1913, prayer was the great weapon in his arsenal, his pathway to the throne of grace. No one who has read what Bounds has written can fail to realize that Edward McKendree Bounds talked with God as a man talks to his friend.

One

A Sacred Privilege

I am the creature of a day, passing through life as an arrow through the air. I am a spirit come from God and returning to God, just hovering over the great gulf, until a few moments hence I am seen no more; I drop into an unchangeable eternity! I want to know one thing: the way to heaven—how to land safe on that happy shore. God Himself has condescended to teach the way; for this end He came from heaven. He has written it down in a book. O give me that book! At any price, give me the Book of God! Lord, is it not Your word, *"If any of you lacks wisdom, let him ask of God, who gives to all liberally and without reproach, and it will be given to him"* (James 1:5)? You give liberally, and do not rebuke. You have said, if any are willing to do Your will, he will know it. I am willing to do; let me know Your will.

—John Wesley

The word *prayer* expresses the largest and most comprehensive approach to God. It gives prominence to the element of devotion. It is communion and communication with God. It is enjoyment of God and access to God.

9

Supplication

Supplication is a more restricted and more intense form of prayer, accompanied by a sense of personal need and limited to the urgent seeking of an answer to a pressing need. Supplication is the very soul of prayer in regard to an intense pleading for something that is greatly needed.

Intercession

Intercession is an enlargement in prayer, a going out in broadness and fullness from self to others. Primarily, it does not center on praying for others, but refers to the freeness, boldness, and childlike confidence of the praying. It is characterized by a complete comfort in the soul's approach to God, unlimited and unhesitating in its access and its demands. This influence and confident trust is to be used for others.

Confiding in the Father

Prayer always, and everywhere, is an immediate confiding approach to, and a request of, God the Father. In the universal and perfect prayer, we see the pattern for all praying: *"Our Father in heaven"* (Matt. 6:9). At the grave of Lazarus, Jesus lifted up His eyes and said, *"Father"* (John 11:41). In His High Priestly Prayer, Jesus again lifted up His eyes to heaven and said, *"Father"* (John 17:1). His praying was personal, familiar, and paternal.

It was also strong, touching, and tearful. Read these words of Paul written about Jesus:

> *Who, in the days of His flesh, when He had offered up prayers and supplications, with vehement cries and tears to Him who was able to save Him from death, and was heard because of His godly fear, though He was a Son, yet He learned obedience by the things which He suffered.* (Heb. 5:7–8)

Asking

In addition, we have asking set forth as prayer: *"If any of you lacks wisdom, let him ask of God, who gives to all liberally and without reproach, and it will be given to him"* (James 1:5). Asking God and receiving from the Lord—direct application to God, immediate connection with God—that is prayer. In First John 5:14–15, we have this statement about prayer:

> *Now this is the confidence that we have in Him, that if we ask anything according to His will, He hears us. And if we know that He hears us, whatever we ask, we know that we have the petitions that we have asked of Him.*

In Philippians 4:6 we find these words about prayer: *"Be anxious for nothing, but in everything by prayer and supplication, with thanksgiving, let your requests be made known to God."*

What Is God's Will about Prayer?

First, it is God's will that we pray. Jesus Christ *"spoke a parable to them, that men always ought to pray and not lose heart"* (Luke 18:1). Paul wrote to young Timothy about the things that God's people are to do, and first among them, he listed prayer: *"I exhort first of all that supplications, prayers, intercessions, and giving of thanks be made for all men"* (1 Tim. 2:1).

In connection with these words Paul declared that the will of God and the redemption and mediation of Jesus Christ for the salvation of all men are all vitally concerned in this matter of prayer. His apostolic authority and solicitude of soul act in harmony with God's will and Christ's intercession to will that *"men pray everywhere"* (v. 8).

Note how frequently prayer is brought forward in the New Testament: *"Continuing steadfastly in prayer"* (Rom. 12:12). *"Pray without ceasing"* (1 Thess. 5:17). *"Continue earnestly in prayer, being vigilant in it with thanksgiving"* (Col. 4:2). *"Be serious and watchful in your prayers"* (1 Pet. 4:7). Christ's clarion call was *"watch and pray"* (Matt. 26:41). What significance do these verses and others have if it is not the will of God that men should pray?

Prayer complements, makes efficient, and cooperates with God's will, whose sovereign sway is to run parallel in extent and power with the atonement of Jesus Christ. Christ, through the eternal Spirit, by the grace of God, *"taste*[d] *death for everyone"* (Heb. 2:9). We, through the eternal Spirit, by the grace of God, pray for every man.

How Can We Know That We Are Praying in the Will of God?

Every true attempt to pray is in response to the will of God. Prayer may be awkward and inarticulate, but it is acceptable to God, because it is offered in obedience to His will. If I will give myself up to the inspiration of the Spirit of God, who commands me to pray, the details and the petitions of that praying will all fall into harmony with the will of Him who wills that I should pray.

What Can Prayer Accomplish?

Prayer is no little thing, no selfish and small matter. It does not concern the petty interests of the person. The littlest prayer expands by the will of God until it touches all words, conserves all interests, and enhances man's greatest wealth and God's greatest good. God is so concerned that men pray that He has promised to answer prayer. He has not promised to do something general if we pray, but He has promised to do the very thing for which we pray.

Prayer, as taught by Jesus in its essential features, enters into all the relations of life. It sanctifies brotherliness. To the Jew, the altar was the symbol and place of prayer. The Jew devoted the altar to the worship of God. Jesus Christ takes the altar of prayer and devotes it to the honor of the brotherhood. How Christ purifies the altar and enlarges it! How He takes it out of the sphere of a mere performance and makes its virtue to consist, not in the mere act of praying, but in the spirit that inspires good actions toward men. Our spirit toward others is affected by a life of prayer. We must be at peace with men (Rom. 12:18), and, if possible, have them at peace with us, before we can be at peace with God. Reconciliation with men is the forerunner of reconciliation with God. (See Matthew 5:22–24.) Our spirit and words must embrace men before they can embrace God. Unity with the brotherhood goes before unity with God.

> *Therefore if you bring your gift to the altar, and there remember that your brother has something against you, leave your gift there before the altar, and go your way. First be reconciled to your brother, and then come and offer your gift.* (Matt. 5:23–24)

Not praying results in lawlessness, discord, and anarchy. Prayer, in the moral government of God, is as strong and far-reaching as the law of gravitation in the material world, and it is as necessary as gravitation to hold things in their proper sphere and in life.

What Is the Value of Prayer?

The space occupied by prayer in the Sermon on the Mount indicates its value to Christ and the importance it holds in His system. Many important principles are discussed in a few verses. The Sermon consists of one hundred and eleven verses, and eighteen are about prayer directly, and others indirectly.

Prayer was one of the chief principles of piety in every dispensation and to every child of God. It did not pertain to the business of Christ to originate duties, but to recover, recast, spiritualize, and reinforce those duties that are essential and original.

With Moses, the great features of prayer were prominent. He never beat the air or fought a false battle. The most serious and strenuous business of his serious and strenuous life was prayer. He prayed often and with intense earnestness of his soul. Intimate as he was with God, his intimacy did not lessen the necessity of prayer. This intimacy only brought clearer insight into the nature and necessity of prayer. It led him to see the greater obligations to pray, and to discover the larger results of praying. In reviewing one of the crises through which Israel passed, when the very existence of the nation was endangered, he wrote: *"I prostrated myself before the LORD; forty days and forty nights I kept prostrating myself"* (Deut. 9:25). Wonderful praying brought wonderful results! Moses knew how to do wonderful praying, and God knew how to give wonderful results.

Can Prayer Change God's Mind?

The collective force of the truths in the Bible are to increase our faith in the doctrine that prayer affects God. It secures favors from God that can be secured in no other way, and which will not be bestowed by God if we do not pray. The whole canon of Bible teaching is to illustrate the great truth that God hears and answers prayer. One of the great purposes of God in His book is to impress upon us indelibly the great importance, the priceless value, and the absolute necessity of asking God for the things that we need. He urges us by every consideration and presses and warns us by every interest. He points us to His own Son as His pledge that prayer will be answered. He teaches us that God is our Father, able to do all things for us and to give all things to us, much more than earthly parents can do or are willing to do for their children (Matt. 7:11; Luke 11:13).

How Can We Pray Well?

Let us thoroughly understand ourselves and this great business of prayer. Our one great business is prayer, and we will never do it well unless we fasten to it all binding force and arrange the best conditions for doing it well. Satan has suffered so much from good praying that all his wily, shrewd, and ensnaring devices will be used to cripple its performance.

We must, by all means, securely attach ourselves to prayer. To be careless in setting a time and place of prayer is to open the door to Satan. To be exact, prompt, unswerving, and careful in even the little things is to buttress ourselves against the Evil One.

Prayer Advances God's Cause

Prayer, by God's own oath (Isa. 56:7), is put in the stones of God's foundations, as eternal as its companion, *"Men always ought to pray"* (Luke

18:1). This is the eternal condition that advances His cause and makes it powerfully aggressive. Men are always to pray for the advance of God's plan. Its strength, beauty, and aggression lie in their prayers. Its power lies simply in the Christian's power to pray. No power is found elsewhere but in the ability to pray. *"My house shall be called a house of prayer for all nations"* (Isa. 56:7). The advance of His kingdom is based on prayer and carried on by the same means.

Prayer Is More Than a Privilege

Prayer is a privilege, a sacred, princely privilege. Prayer is a duty, an obligation most binding and most imperative, that should hold us to it. But prayer is more than a privilege, more than a duty. It is a means, an instrument, a condition. Not to pray is to lose much more than to fail in the exercise and enjoyment of a high, sweet privilege. Not to pray is to fail along lines far more important than even the violation of an obligation.

Prayer Accesses God's Help

Prayer is the appointed condition of receiving God's aid. This aid is as manifold and infinite as God's ability; it is as varied and inexhaustible as man's need. Prayer is the avenue through which God supplies man's needs. Prayer is the channel through which all good flows from God to man, and from men to men. God is the Christian's Father. Asking and giving are found in that relationship.

Prayer Ennobles the One Who Prays

Man is the one more immediately concerned in this great work of praying. It ennobles man's reason to employ it in prayer. The office and work of prayer is the divinest engagement of man's reason. Prayer makes man's reason to shine. Intelligence of the highest order approves prayer. He is the wisest man who prays the most and the best. Prayer is the school of wisdom as well as of piety.

Prayer is not a picture to handle, to admire, to look at. It is not beauty, coloring, shape, attitude, imagination, or genius. These things do not pertain to its character or conduct. It is not poetry or music. Its inspiration and melody come from heaven. Prayer belongs to the spirit, and at times it possesses the spirit and stirs the spirit with high and holy purposes and resolves.

Two

Man's Poverty and God's Riches

> For two hours I struggled on, forsaken of God, and met neither God nor man, all one chilly afternoon. When at last, standing still and looking at Schiehallion[*] clothed in white from top to bottom, these words of David shot up into my heart: *"Wash me, and I shall be whiter than snow"* (Ps. 51:7). In a moment I was with God, or rather God was with me. I walked home with my heart in a flame of fire. —Alexander Whyte

We have much fine writing and learned talk about the subjective benefits of prayer—how prayer secures its full measure of results, not by affecting God, but by affecting us, by becoming a training school for those who pray. We are taught by such teachers that the province of prayer is not to get, but to train. Prayer thus becomes a mere performance, a drill sergeant, a school in which patience, tranquility, and dependence are taught. In this school, denial of petitions is the most valuable teacher. However well all this may look, and

---

[*] Schiehallion, with an elevation of 3,553 feet, is a mountain in Central Scotland.

however reasonable it may seem, there is nothing of it in the Bible. The clear and often repeated language of the Bible is that prayer is to be answered by God, that God occupies the relation of a father to us, and that as our Father He gives to us the things for which we ask. The best praying, therefore, is the praying that receives an answer.

The Significance of Prayer

The possibilities and necessity of prayer are carved on the eternal foundations of the Gospel. The relationship that is established between the Father and the Son and the decreed covenant between the two, have prayer as the base of their existence. Prayer is the condition of the advance and success of the Gospel. Prayer is the condition by which all foes are to be overcome and all the inheritance is to be possessed.

Moses
Joshua
Jesus
Paul

These are self-evident truths, though they may be very familiar ones. But these are the times when biblical principles need to be stressed, pressed, and reiterated. The very air is rife with influences, practices, and theories that sap foundations, and the most veritable truths and the most self-evident axioms go down by insidious and invisible attacks.

The Work of Prayer

Additionally, the tendency of these times is to an ostentatious parade of doing what enfeebles the life and dissipates the spirit of praying. There may be kneeling, and there may be standing in prayerful attitude. There may be much bowing of the head, and yet there may be no serious, real praying. Prayer is real work. Praying is vital work. Prayer has in its keeping the very heart of worship. There may be the exhibit, the circumstance, and the pomp of praying, and yet no real praying. There may be much attitude, gesture, and verbiage, but no praying.

The School of Prayer

Who can come into God's presence in prayer? Who can come before the great God, *"Maker of all things"* (Jer. 10:16), *"the God and Father of our Lord Jesus Christ"* (Col. 1:3), who holds in His hands all good, and who is all-powerful and able to do all things? For man to approach this great God, what lowliness, truth, cleanness of hands, and purity of heart are needed and demanded!

Throughout the Bible, we are impressed that it is more important and urgent that men pray than that they be skilled in the sermonizing teachings about prayer. (See, for example, Matthew 6:6–7; Luke 18:10–14.) Prayer is a thing of the heart, not of the schools. It is more about feeling than about words. Praying is the best school in which to learn to pray; prayer is the best dictionary to define the art and nature of praying.

I repeat: Prayer is not a mere habit, riveted by custom and memory, something that must be gone through with, its value depending upon the decency and perfection of the performance. Prayer is not a duty that must be performed to ease obligation and to quiet conscience. Prayer is not a mere privilege, a sacred indulgence to be taken advantage of at leisure, at pleasure, or at will, with no serious loss attending its omission.

The Results of Prayer

Prayer is a solemn service due to God, an adoration, a worship, an approach to God for some request, the presenting of some desire, the expression of some need to Him, who supplies all need, and who satisfies all desires; who, as a Father, finds His greatest pleasure in relieving the needs and granting the desires of His children. Prayer is the child's request, not to the winds or to the world, but to the Father. Prayer is the outstretched arms of the child for the Father's help. Prayer is the child's cry calling to the Father's ear, the Father's heart, and the Father's ability. Prayer is the cry that the Father is to hear, the Father is to feel, and the Father is to relieve. Prayer is the seeking of God's great and greatest good that will not come if we do not pray.

Prayer is an ardent and believing cry to God for some specific thing. God's rule is to answer by giving the specific thing asked for. With it may come much of other gifts and graces. Strength, serenity, sweetness, and faith may come as the bearers of the gifts. But even they come because God hears and answers prayer.

We are following the plain letter and spirit of the Bible when we affirm that God answers prayer, and answers by giving us the very things we desire, and that the withholding of what we desire and the giving of something else is not the rule, but rare and exceptional. When His children cry for bread, He gives them bread. (See Matthew 7:9–11; Luke 11:3, 11–13.)

The Definition of Prayer

Revelation does not deal in philosophical subtleties, verbal niceties, or hairsplitting distinctions. It unfolds relationships, declares principles, and enforces duties. The heart must define; the experience must realize. Paul came on the stage too late to define prayer. What had been so well done by patriarchs and prophets needed no return to dictionaries. Christ is Himself the illustration and definition of prayer. He prayed as man had never prayed. He put prayer on a higher basis, with grander results and simpler being than it had ever known. He taught Paul how to pray by the revelation of Himself, which is the first call to prayer, and the first lesson in praying. Prayer, like love, is too ethereal and too heavenly to be held in the coarse arms of cold definitions. It belongs to heaven, and to the heart, not to words and ideas only.

Prayer is no petty invention of man, a contrived relief for imagined ills. Prayer is no dreary performance, dead and death-dealing, but is God's enabling act for man, living and life-giving, joy and joy-giving. Prayer is the contact of a living soul with God. In prayer, God stoops to kiss man, to bless man, and to assist man in everything that God can devise or man can need. Prayer fills man's emptiness with God's fullness. It fills man's poverty with God's riches. It replaces man's weakness with God's strength. It banishes man's littleness with God's greatness. Prayer is God's plan to supply man's great and continuous need with God's great and continuous abundance.

The Power of Prayer

What is this prayer to which men are called? It is not a mere form, a child's play. It is serious, difficult work, the manliest, the mightiest, the most divine work that man can do. Prayer lifts men out of the earthly and links them with the heavenly. Men are never nearer heaven, nearer God, never more Godlike, never in deeper sympathy and truer partnership with Jesus Christ, than when praying. Love, philanthropy, holy confidences—all of them helpful and tender for men—are born and perfected by prayer.

Prayer is not merely a question of duty, but of salvation. Are men saved who are not men of prayer? Is not the gift, the inclination, the habit of prayer one of the elements or characteristics of salvation? Can it be possible to be in affinity with Jesus Christ and not be prayerful? Is it possible to have the Holy Spirit and not have the spirit of prayer? Can one have the new birth and not be born to prayer? Are not the life of the Spirit and the life of prayer coordinate and consistent? Can brotherly love be in the heart that is unschooled in prayer?

The Forms of Prayer

We have two kinds of prayer named in the New Testament: prayer and supplication. Prayer denotes prayer in general. Supplication is a more intense and special form of prayer. These two should be combined. Then we would have devotion in its widest and sweetest form, and supplication with its most earnest and personal sense of need.

In Paul's Prayer Directory, found in the sixth chapter of Ephesians, we are taught to be always in prayer, as we are always in the battle. (See verses 10–18.) The Holy Spirit is to be sought by intense supplication, and our supplications are to be charged by His vitalizing, illuminating, and ennobling energy. Watchfulness is to fit us for this intense praying and intense fighting. Perseverance is an essential element in successful praying, as in every other realm of conflict. The saints universal are to be helped on to victory by the aid of our prayers. Apostolic courage, ability, and success are to be gained by the prayers of the soldier-saints everywhere.

The Intelligence of Prayer

It is only those of deep and true vision who can administer prayer. In Revelation 4:6, 8, the *"living creatures"* are described as *"full of eyes in front and in back"* and *"full of eyes around and within."* Eyes are for seeing. Clearness, intensity, and perfection of sight are in prayer. Vigilance and profound insight are in it, the faculty of knowing.

25

It is by prayer that the eyes of our hearts are opened. (See Ephesians 1:15–19.) Clear, profound knowledge of the mysteries of grace is secured by prayer. These *"living creatures"* had eyes *"around and within."* They were *"full of eyes."* The highest form of life is intelligent. Ignorance is degrading and low, in the spiritual realm as it is in other realms. Prayer gives us eyes to see God. Prayer is seeing God. The prayer life is knowledge without and within. All vigilance without, all vigilance within. There can be no intelligent prayer without knowledge within. Our inner condition and our inner needs must be felt and known.

It takes prayer to minister. It takes the highest form of life to minister. Prayer is the highest intelligence; the profoundest wisdom; the most vital, the most joyous, the most efficacious, the most powerful of all vocations. It is life, radiant, transporting, eternal life. Away with dry forms, with dead, cold habits of prayer! Away with sterile routine and with senseless performances in prayer! Let us get at the serious work, the chief business, of men, that of prayer. Let us work at it skillfully. Let us seek to be adept in this great work of praying. Let us be master workmen in this high art of praying. Let us be in the habit of prayer, so devoted to prayer, so filled with its rich spices, so ardent by its holy flame, that all heaven and earth will be perfumed by its aroma, and nations will be blessed by our prayers. Heaven will be fuller and brighter in glorious inhabitants, earth will be better prepared for its bridal day, and hell robbed of many of its victims, because we have lived to pray.

The Standard of Prayer

There is not only a sad and ruinous neglect of any attempt to pray, but also an immense waste in the apparent praying that is done, such as formal prayers or repetitious prayers. Men cleave to the form and semblance of a thing after the heart and reality have gone out of it. This truth finds illustrations in many who seem to pray. Formal praying has a strong hold and a strong following.

For example, Eli thought that Hannah was not really praying because he saw her lips moving but could not hear any sound (1 Sam. 1:12–13). He urged her, *"Put your wine away!"* (v. 14). He thought she was guilty of hypocrisy. Her prayer, though, was sincere, and she answered Eli's accusations by saying, *"I have drunk neither wine nor intoxicating drink, but have poured out my soul before the LORD"* (v. 15). God's serious promise to the Jews was, *"Then you will call upon Me and go and pray to Me, and I will listen to you. And you will seek Me and find Me, when you search for Me with all your heart"* (Jer. 29:12–13).

Let all present-day praying be measured by these standards: pouring out our souls before God and seeking Him with all our hearts. How much prayer will be found to be mere form, waste, and worthless in light of these standards? James said of Elijah that he *"prayed earnestly"* (James 5:17).

In Paul's directions to Timothy about prayer (1 Tim. 2:1–2), we have a comprehensive description of prayer in its different types or manifestations.

They are all in the plural form: *"supplications, prayers, intercessions"* (v. 1). They reveal the many-sidedness, the endless diversity, and the necessity of going beyond the formal simplicity of a single prayer. They show the need to deliberately add prayer upon prayer, supplication to supplication, and intercession to intercession, until the combined force of prayers in their most excellent forms unite their power to our praying. Unlimited excellence and continuous accumulation of prayer in its various forms are the only measures of prayer. The term *prayer* is the common and comprehensive description for the act, the duty, the spirit, and the service of our various interactions with God. It is our condensed word for worship. The element of prayer is not as conspicuous in heavenly worship; prayer is the conspicuous, all-important essence, and all-coloring ingredient of earthly worship, while praise is the preeminent, comprehensive, all-coloring, and all-inspiring element of heavenly worship.

Three

The Essence of Earthly Worship

> Where the spiritual consciousness is concerned—
> the department that asks the question and
> demands the evidence—no evidence is competent
> or relevant except such as is spiritual. Only that
> which is above matter and above logic can be
> heard, because the very question at issue is the
> existence and personality of a spiritual and
> supernatural God. Only *"the Spirit Himself bears
> witness with our spirit"* (Rom. 8:16). This must
> be done in a spiritual or supernatural way, or it
> cannot be done at all. —C. L. Chilton

The Jewish law and the prophets knew something of God as a Father. They had comforting glimpses, although occasional and imperfect, of the great truth of God's Fatherhood and our sonship. Christ lays the foundation of prayer deep and strong with this basic principle: the law of prayer, the right to pray, rests on sonship. Saying *"Our Father"* (Matt. 6:9) brings us into the closest relationship to God. Prayer is the child's approach, the child's plea, the child's right. The law of prayer involves looking up; we must lift our eyes to *"our*

Father in heaven" (v. 9). Our Father's house is our home in heaven. Both heavenly citizenship and heavenly homesickness are found in prayer. Prayer is an appeal from the lowness, the emptiness, the need of earth to the highness, the fullness, and the all-sufficiency of heaven. Prayer turns the eye and the heart heavenward with a child's longings, a child's trust, and a child's expectancy. To hallow God's name, to speak it with bated breath, to hold it sacredly—this also belongs to prayer.

The Way to Salvation

It is requisite to dictate to children the necessity of prayer in order to secure their salvation. Unhappily, it is thought sufficient to tell them there is a heaven and a hell, that they must avoid the latter place and seek to reach the former. Yet they are not taught the easiest way to arrive at salvation. The only way to heaven is by the route of prayer. Everyone is capable of such prayers of the heart. Prayer that leads to heaven is not reasonings that are the fruit of study or exercises of the imagination that fill the mind with puzzling thoughts but that fail to settle salvation. The simple, confidential prayer of the child to his Father is the way to heaven.

The Attitude of Prayer

Poverty of spirit enters into true praying. *"Blessed are the poor in spirit, for theirs is the kingdom of heaven"* (Matt. 5:3). *"The poor"* means paupers or beggars, those who live on the bounties of others. Christ's people live by asking. Prayer is the Christian's vital breath. It is his affluent inheritance, his daily annuity.

The Need for Prayer

By His own example, Christ illustrated the nature and necessity of prayer. Everywhere He declared that he who is on God's mission in this world will pray. He is an illustrious example of the principle that the more devoted the man is to God, the more prayerful he will be. The more of the Spirit of the Father and of the Son a man has, the more prayerful he will be. Conversely, it is true that the more prayerful he is, the more of the Spirit of the Father and of the Son he will receive.

At the great events and crowning periods of the life of Jesus, we find Him in prayer—at the beginning of His ministry (John 2:1–11); at the fords of the Jordan, when the Holy Spirit descended upon Him (Luke 3:21–22); just prior to the Transfiguration (Luke 9:28–36); and in the Garden of Gethsemane (Matt. 26:36–46). The words of Peter apply here well: *"Christ also suffered for us, leaving us an example, that* [we] *should follow His steps"* (1 Pet. 2:21).

The Progressive Nature of Prayer

There is an important principle of prayer found in some of the miracles of Christ. It is the progressive nature of the answer to prayer. God does not always give the full answer to prayer at once, but rather progressively, step by step. Mark described a case that illustrates this important truth that is too often overlooked:

> *Then* [Jesus] *came to Bethsaida; and they brought a blind man to Him, and begged Him to touch him. So He took the blind man by the hand and led him out of the town. And when He had spit on his eyes and put His hands on him, He asked him if he saw anything. And He looked up and said, "I see men like trees, walking." Then He put His hands on his eyes again and made him look up. And he was restored and saw everyone clearly.* (Mark 8:22–25)

At times, He has to take us aside from the world, where He can have us all to Himself, and there speak to and deal with us.

God Works in His Own Way

Three cures for blindness demonstrated in the ministry of our Lord illustrate the nature of God's working in answering prayer and show the inexhaustible variety and omnipotence of His working.

In the first case Christ came incidentally on a blind man at Jerusalem (John 9:1). Jesus made clay, softened it with saliva, and smeared it on the eyes of the blind man (v. 6). Then He commanded the man, *"Go, wash in the pool of Siloam"* (v. 7).

The gracious results lay at the end of his obedient washing. The failure to go and wash would have been fatal to the cure. No one, not even the blind man, in this instance, requested the cure. (See John 9:1–38.)

In the second case the parties who bring the blind man to Jesus back their bringing with earnest prayer for his cure; they beseech Christ to simply touch him, as though their faith would relieve the burden of a heavy operation (Mark 8:22). But Jesus *"took the blind man by the hand and led him out of the town"* (v. 23). Alone, in secret, apart from the crowd, this work was to be done. Jesus spat *"on his eyes and put His hands on him"* (v. 23). The response was not complete; there was a dawning of light, a partial recovery (v. 24). The first gracious communication gave him a disordered vision, but the second stroke perfected the cure (v. 25). The man's submissive faith in giving himself up to Christ to be led away alone to a private spot was a prominent feature of his cure, as were the gradual reception of sight, and the necessity of a second touch to finish the work.

The third was the case of blind Bartimaeus. (See Mark 10:46–52.) His healing demonstrated the urgency of his faith. He declared his need in clamorous utterances that were rebuked by those who were following Christ. The warnings to be quiet only intensified the man's efforts and emboldened him. Despite the opposition, *"he cried out all the more, 'Son of David, have mercy on me!'"* (v. 48). Jesus restored Bartimaeus' sight and told him, *"Your faith has made you well"* (v. 52).

The first case came on Christ unawares; the second was brought with specific intent to Him. The last went after Christ with irresistible urgency and was met by the resistance of the multitude and the seeming indifference of Christ. The cure, though, was without the interposition of any agent—no taking by the hand, no gentle or severe touch, no spittle or clay or washing—a word only and his sight, full-orbed, came instantly. Each one experienced the same divine power, the same blessed results, but with marked diversity in the expression of their faith and the mode of their cure. Suppose the first had set up the particulars and process of his cure—the spittle, the clay, the washing in Siloam—as the only divine process, as the only genuine credentials of a divine work. How far from the truth, how narrow and misleading, would such a standard of decision have been! Not methods, but results, are the tests of the divine work.

Each one could say, *"One thing I know: that though I was blind, now I see"* (John 9:25). The results were conscious results. They knew that Christ did the work. Faith was the instrument, but it was exercised in different ways. The method of Christ's working was different; the various steps that brought them to the gracious end on their parts and on His part were strikingly dissimilar at many points.

Questions for Consideration

What are the limitations of prayer? How far do its benefits and possibilities reach? What part of God's dealing with man, and with man's world, is unaffected by prayer? Do the possibilities of prayer cover all temporal and spiritual good? The answers to these questions are of transcendental importance. The answers will gauge the effort and results of our praying. The answers will greatly enhance the value of prayer, or will greatly depress prayer. The answers to these important questions are fully covered by Paul's words on prayer: *"Be anxious for nothing, but in everything by prayer and supplication, with thanksgiving, let your requests be made known to God"* (Phil. 4:6).

Then you will call upon Me and go and pray to Me, and I will listen to you. And you will seek Me and find Me, when you search for Me with all your heart.

—Jeremiah 29:12–13

When you pray, go into your room, and when you have shut your door, pray to your Father who is in the secret place; and your Father who sees in secret will reward you openly.   —Matthew 6:6

Be anxious for nothing, but in everything by prayer and supplication, with thanksgiving, let your requests be made known to God.   —Philippians 4:6

Four

God's Part in Prayer

Christ is all. We are complete in Him. He is the answer to every need, the perfect Savior. He needs no decoration to heighten His beauty, no prop to increase His stability, no girding to perfect His strength. Who can gild refined gold, whiten the snow, perfume the rose, or heighten the colors of the summer sunset? Who will prop the mountains or help the great deep? It is not Christ and philosophy or Christ and money or civilization or diplomacy or science or organization. It is Christ alone. He trod *"the winepress alone"* (Isa. 63:3). *"His own arm brought salvation"* (Isa. 59:16). He is enough. He is the comfort, the strength, the wisdom, the righteousness, the sanctification of all men.   —C. L. Chilton

Use as an opening for Sermon

Prayer is God's business to which men can attend. Prayer is God's necessary business that only men can do, and that men must do. Men who belong to God are obliged to pray. They are not obliged to grow rich or to make money. They are not obliged to have large success in business. These activities are incidental, occasional, merely nominal, as far as integrity to heaven and loyalty to God are concerned. Material successes are immaterial to God. Men are neither better nor worse with those things or without them. They are not sources of reputation or elements of character in the heavenly estimates. But to pray, to really pray, is the source of revenue, the basis of reputation, and the element of character in the estimation of God. Men are obliged to pray as they are obliged to be Christlike. Prayer is loyalty to God. Not to pray is to reject Christ and to abandon heaven. A life of prayer is the only life that heaven counts.

✱ Prayer Releases God's Promises

God is vitally concerned that men should pray. Men are bettered by praying, and the world is bettered by prayer. God does His best work for the world through prayer. God's greatest glory and man's highest good are secured by prayer. Prayer forms the godliest men and the godliest world.

God's promises lie like giant corpses without life, headed for decay and dust, unless people appropriate and give life to these promises through earnest and prevailing prayer.

Promise is like the unsown seed, the germ of life in it, but the soil and culture of prayer are necessary to germinate and culture the seed. Prayer is God's life-giving breath. God's purposes move along the pathway made by prayer to their glorious designs. God's purposes are always moving to their high and gracious ends, but the movement is along the way marked by unceasing prayer. The breath of prayer in man is from God.

✱ Prayer Changes the One Who Prays

God has everything to do with prayer, as well as everything to do with the one who prays. To him who prays, and as he prays, the hour is sacred because it is God's hour. The experience is sacred because it is the soul's approach to God, and a time of dealing with God. No hour is more hallowed, because it is the occasion of the soul's mightiest approach to God and brings the fullest revelation from God. Men are Godlike and men are blessed, inasmuch as the hour of prayer has the most of God in it. Prayer makes and measures the approach to God. He knows not God who knows not how to pray. He has never seen God whose eye has not been seeking for God in the prayer closet. God can be seen in the private place of prayer. His dwelling place is in secret. *"He who dwells in the secret place of the Most High shall abide under the shadow of the Almighty"* (Ps. 91:1).

✱ He has never studied God who has not had his intellect broadened, strengthened, clarified, and uplifted by prayer. Almighty God commands prayer. God waits on prayer to order His ways, and God delights in prayer. To God, prayer is what incense was to the Jewish temple. It impregnates everything, perfumes everything, and sweetens everything.

✱ Prayer Accomplishes God's Purposes

The possibilities of prayer cover the whole purposes of God through Christ. God conditions all gifts in all dispensations to His Son. *"Ask of Me,"* God the Father said to the Son, as that Son was moving earthward on the stupendous enterprise for a world's salvation, *"and I will give You the nations for Your inheritance, and the ends of the earth for Your possession"* (Ps. 2:8). Hinging on prayer were all the means, results, and successes of that wonderful and divine movement for man's salvation. Broad and profound, mysterious and wonderful, was the scheme.

Prayer Draws Us Closer to God

The answer to prayer is assured not only by the promises of God, but also by God's relation to us as a Father.

But you, when you pray, go into your room, and when you have shut your door, pray to your Father who is in the secret place; and your Father who sees in secret will reward you openly. (Matt. 6:6)

Again, we have these words:

If you then, being evil, know how to give good gifts to your children, how much more will your Father who is in heaven give good things to those who ask Him! (Matt. 7:11)

Prayer Increases Confidence in Asking

God encourages us to pray, not only by the certainty of the answer, but also by the generosity of the promise, and the bounty of the Giver. How princely the promise! *"And whatever things you ask in prayer, believing, you will receive"* (Matt. 21:22). Then add to that *"whatever"* this promise: *"If you ask **anything** in My name, I will do it"* (John 14:14, emphasis added). That verse covers all things, without qualification, exception, or limitation. The word *"anything"* expands and makes specific the promise. The challenge of God to us is, *"Call to Me, and I will answer you, and show you great and mighty things, which you do not know"* (Jer. 33:3). This includes, like the answer to Solomon's prayer (see 1 Kings 3:5–14), what was specifically prayed for, but embraces vastly more of great value and of great necessity.

Almighty God seems to fear we will hesitate to ask largely, apprehensive that we will strain His ability. He declares that He is *"able to do exceedingly abundantly above all that we ask or think"* (Eph. 3:20). He almost paralyzes us by giving us a carte blanche, *"Ask Me of things to come concerning My sons; and concerning the work of My hands, you command Me"* (Isa. 45:11). How He charges, commands, and urges us to pray! He goes beyond promise and says, *"God so loved the world that He gave His only begotten Son"* (John 3:16). *"He who did not spare His own Son, but delivered Him up for us all, how shall He not with Him also freely give us all things?"* (Rom. 8:32).

God gave us *"all things"* in prayer by promise because He had given us "all things" in His Son. What an amazing gift—His Son! Prayer is as immeasurable as His own blessed Son. There is

41

nothing on earth or in heaven, for time or eternity, that God's Son did not secure for us. By prayer, God gives us the vast and matchless inheritance that is ours by virtue of His Son. God charges us to *"come boldly to the throne of grace"* (Heb. 4:16). God is glorified and Christ is honored by large asking.

Prayer Is a Part of God's Plan

What is true of the promises of God is equally true of the purposes of God. We might say that God does nothing without prayer. His most gracious purposes are conditioned on prayer. His marvelous promises in the thirty-sixth chapter of Ezekiel are subject to this qualification and condition. *"Thus says the Lord GOD: 'I will also let the house of Israel inquire of Me to do this for them'"* (v. 37).

In Psalm 2 the purposes of God to His enthroned Christ are enjoined by prayer. The decree that promises to Him the nations for His inheritance relies on prayer for its fulfillment: *"Ask of Me"* (v. 8). We see how sadly the decree has failed in its operation, not because of the weakness of God's purpose, but by the weakness of man's praying. It takes God's mighty decree and man's mighty praying to bring to pass these glorious results.

In the Seventy-second Psalm we have an insight into the mighty power of prayer as the force that God moves on the conquest of Christ: *"Prayer also will be made for Him continually"* (v. 15). In this statement Christ's movements are put into the hands of prayer.

When Christ, with a sad and sympathizing heart, looked upon the ripened fields of humanity and saw the great need for laborers, His purposes were for more laborers, and so He charged His disciples, *"Pray the Lord of the harvest to send out laborers into His harvest"* (Matt. 9:38).

Paul reminded the believers of the eternal purposes of God, and how he bowed his knees to God in order that His eternal purpose might be accomplished (Eph. 2:8–3:19), and that they might *"be filled with all the fullness of God"* (v. 19).

We see in Job how God made His purposes for Job's three friends conditional on Job's praying, and God's purposes in regard to Job were brought about by the same means. (See Job 42:8–13.)

The relationship and necessity of saintly prayers to God's plans and operations in executing the salvation of men are set forth in rich, expressive symbol, wherein the angels are involved in the prayers of the saints (Rev. 8:3–4).

Prayer gives efficiency and utility to the promises. The mighty ongoing of God's purposes rests on prayer. The representatives of the church in heaven and of all creation before the throne of God have *"golden bowls full of incense, which are the prayers of the saints"* (Rev. 5:8).

Prayer Is Based on a Relationship

We have said before that prayer is based not simply on a promise, but on a relationship. The returning, penitent sinner's prayer is based on a promise. The child of God's prayer is founded on his relationship to his heavenly Father. What the earthly father has belongs to the child for present and prospective uses. The child asks; the father gives. The relationship is one of asking and answering, of giving and receiving. The child is dependent on the father, must look to the father, must ask of the father, and must receive of the father.

We know how with earthly parents asking and giving are inherent in the parent-child relationship, and how in the very act of asking and giving, the relationship of parent and child is cemented, sweetened, and enriched. The parent finds his wealth of pleasure and satisfaction in giving to an obedient child, and the child finds his wealth in the father's loving and continuous giving.

It must be kept in mind that there is no test of our being in the family of God that is surer than this thing of prayer. God's children pray. They rest in Him for all things. They ask Him for all things—for everything. The faith of the child in the father is evinced by the child's asking. It is the answer to prayer that convinces men not only that there is a God, but also that He is a God who concerns Himself about men and about the affairs of this world. Answered prayer brings God near and assures men of His being. Answered prayers are the credentials of our relationship to, and our representation of, Him. Men cannot represent God who do not receive answers to prayer from Him.

The possibilities of prayer are found in the unlimited promise, the willingness, and the power of God to answer prayer, to answer all prayer, to answer every prayer, and to supply fully the immeasurable needs of man. <u>None is so needy as man, none is so able and anxious to supply every need and any need as God.</u>

Prayer Is Powerful

Prayer affects God more powerfully than His own purposes. God's will, words, and purposes are all subject to review when the mighty power of prayer comes in. How mighty prayer is with God may be seen as He readily sets aside His own fixed and declared purposes in answer to prayer. The whole plan of salvation would have been blocked had Jesus Christ prayed for the twelve legions of angels to carry dismay and ruin to His enemies. (See Matthew 26:53.)

The fasting and prayers of the Ninevites changed God's purpose to destroy that wicked city (see Jonah 3:1–10), after Jonah had gone there and cried unto the people, *"Yet forty days, and Nineveh shall be overthrown!"* (v. 4).

Jesus Sets the Example in Prayer

Almighty God is concerned in our praying. He wills it, He commands it, He inspires it. Jesus Christ in heaven is always praying for us (Heb. 7:25). Prayer is His law and His life. The Holy Spirit teaches us how to pray. He prays for us *"with groanings which cannot be uttered"* (Rom. 8:26). All these examples show the deep concern of

God in prayer. They reveal very clearly how vital prayer is to His work in this world, and how far-reaching are its possibilities. Prayer is at the very center of the heart and will of God concerning men. *"Rejoice always, pray without ceasing, in everything give thanks; for this is the will of God in Christ Jesus for you"* (1 Thess. 5:16–18). Prayer is the polestar around which rejoicing and thanksgiving revolve. Prayer is the heart sending its full and happy pulsations up to God through the glad currents of joy and thanksgiving.

Prayer Brings Amazing Results

By prayer God's name is hallowed. By prayer God's kingdom comes. By prayer is His kingdom established in power and made to move with conquering force swifter than light. By prayer God's will is done until earth rivals heaven in harmony and beauty. By prayer daily labor is sanctified and enriched; pardon is secured, and Satan is defeated. Prayer concerns God and concerns man in every way.

God has nothing too good to give in answer to prayer. There is no vengeance pronounced by God so dire that does not yield to prayer. There is no justice so flaming that is not quenched by prayer.

Take the record and attitude of heaven concerning Saul of Tarsus. That attitude is changed and that record is erased when the astonishing condition is announced, *"Behold, he is praying"* (Acts 9:11).

The cowardly Jonah was alive, and on dry ground, with scarcely the taste of the sea or the smell of its weeds about him, when he prayed:

Out of the belly of Sheol I cried, and You heard my voice....The waters surrounded me, even to my soul; the deep closed around me; weeds were wrapped around my head. I went down to the moorings of the mountains; the earth with its bars closed behind me forever; yet You have brought up my life from the pit, O LORD, my God. When my soul fainted within me, I remembered the LORD; and my prayer went up to You, into Your holy temple....So the LORD spoke to the fish, and it vomited Jonah onto dry land.

(Jonah 2:2, 5–7, 10)

Prayer has all the force of God in it. Prayer can get anything that God has. Thus prayer has all of its plea and its claim in the name of Jesus Christ, and there is nothing too good or great for God to give that name.

The Salvation of Souls Relies on Prayer

Preaching should no more fully declare and fulfill the will of God for the salvation of all men, than should the prayers of God's saints declare the same great truth, as they wrestle in their prayer closets for this sublime end. God's heart is set on the salvation of all men. This concerns God. He has declared this truth in the death of His Son by

47

an unspeakable voice, and every movement on earth for this end pleases God. And so He declares that our prayers for the salvation of all men are well pleasing in His sight. The sublime and holy inspiration of pleasing God should ever move us to pray for all men. God eyes the prayer closet, and nothing we can do pleases Him better than our sympathetic, ardent praying for all men. It is the embodiment and test of our devotion to God's will and of our sympathetic loyalty to God.

The apostle Paul did not descend to a weak argument, but pressed the necessity of prayer by the most forceful facts. Jesus Christ, the God-man, the highest illustration of manhood, is the *"Mediator between God and men"* (1 Tim. 2:5). Jesus died for all men. His life is an intercession for all men. His death is a prayer for all men. On earth, Jesus Christ knew no higher law, no holier business, no diviner life, than to plead for men. In heaven He knows no more royal estate, no higher theme, than to intercede for men. On earth He lived and prayed and died for men. His life, His death, and His exaltation in heaven all plead for men.

Is there any work, any higher work, for the disciple to do than His Lord did? Is there any loftier employment, more honorable, more divine, than to pray for men? Is there anything more important than to take their woes, their sins, and their perils before God—to be one with Christ? Can we neglect to pray when prayer can break the chains that bind them and the hell that holds them, and lift them to immortality and eternal life?

Five

The Divine Teacher of Prayer

[A man knocks on the door of his neighbor's house and says,] "A friend of mine in his journey has come to me, and I have nothing to set before him!" He knocks again. "Friend! lend me three loaves." He waits a while and then knocks again. "Friend! I must have three loaves!" "Trouble me not: the door is now shut; I cannot rise and give thee!" He stands still. He turns to go home; He comes back. He knocks again. "Friend!" he cries. He puts his ear to the door. There is a sound inside, and then the light of a candle shines through the hole of the door. The bars of the door are drawn back, and he gets not three loaves only, but as many as he needs. *"So I say to you, ask, and it will be given to you; seek, and you will find; knock, and it will be opened to you"* (Luke 11:9).

—Alexander Whyte

J esus Christ was the divine Teacher of prayer. Its power and nature had been illustrated by many saints and prophets in olden times, but modern sainthood and modern teachers of prayer had lost their inspiration and life. Religiously dead, teachers and superficial ecclesiastics had forgotten what it was to pray. They recited many prayers on state occasions, in public meetings, with much ostentation and parade, but they did not pray. To them it was almost a lost practice. In the multiplicity of "saying prayers," they had lost the art of praying.

The Serious Effects of Neglecting Prayer

The history of the disciples during the earthly life of our Lord was not marked by much devotion. They were enamored by their personal association with Christ. They were charmed by His words, excited by His miracles, and entertained and concerned by the hopes that a selfish interest aroused in His person and mission. Taken up with superficial and worldly views of His character, they neglected and overlooked the deeper and weightier things that belonged to Him and His mission. The neglect of the most obligatory and ordinary duties by them was a noticeable feature in their actions. So evident and singular was their conduct in this regard that it became a matter of grave inquiry on one occasion and severe chiding on another.

The scribes and Pharisees said to Jesus:

> *"Why do the disciples of John fast often and make prayers, and likewise those of the Pharisees, but Yours eat and drink?" And He said to them, "Can you make the friends of the bridegroom fast while the bridegroom is with them? But the days will come when the bridegroom will be taken away from them; then they will fast in those days."*
>
> (Luke 5:33–35)

The Divine Teacher of Prayer

Jesus Teaches the Importance of Prayer

In the example and teaching of Jesus Christ, prayer assumes its proper relationship to God's person, God's movements, and God's Son. Jesus Christ was essentially the Teacher of prayer by precept and example. We have glimpses of His praying that, like indices, tell how full of prayer the pages, chapters, and volumes of His life were. The summation that covers not just one segment, but the whole circle of His life and character, is preeminently that of prayer! *"In the days of His flesh,"* the divine Record reads, *"...He...offered up prayers and supplications, with vehement cries and tears"* (Heb. 5:7). He was the most earnest of all who have prayed or will pray, the Intercessor of all intercessors. He approached God with humility, and He supplicated with strongest pleas.

Jesus Christ taught the importance of prayer when He urged His disciples to pray. But He shows us more than that. He shows how far prayer enters into the purposes of God. We must always keep in mind that the relationship of Jesus Christ to God is the relationship of asking and giving, the Son ever asking, the Father ever giving. We must never forget that God has put the conquering, inheriting, and expanding forces of Christ's cause into prayer. *"Ask of Me, and I will give You the nations for Your inheritance, and the ends of the earth for Your possession"* (Ps. 2:8).

"Ask of Me" embodied the royal proclamation and the universal condition when the Son was enthroned as the world's Mediator, and when He

was sent on His mission of receiving grace and power. We very naturally learn from these examples how Jesus stressed praying as the sole condition of His receiving His possession and inheritance.

✳ Prayer Has No Boundaries

Necessarily in this study on prayer, lines of thought will cross each other, and the same Scripture passage or incident will be mentioned more than once, simply because a passage may teach one or more truths. This is the case when we speak of the vast comprehensiveness of prayer. How all-inclusive Jesus Christ makes prayer! It has no limitations in extent or things! The promises to prayer are Godlike in their magnificence, wideness, and universality. In their nature these promises, inspiration, creation, and results have to do with God. Who but Jesus could say, *"Whatever things you ask in prayer, believing, you will receive"* (Matt. 21:22)? Who can command and direct *"whatever things"* but God? Neither man nor chance nor the law of results are so far lifted above change, limitations, or condition, or have in them mighty forces that can direct and cause all things, as to promise the bestowment and direction of all things.

Parables and incidents from life were used by Christ to emphasize the necessity and importance of prayer. His miracles are but parables of prayer. In nearly all of them prayer figures distinctly, and some features of it are illustrated. The Syro-Phoenician woman is a preeminent illustration of the ability and the success of perseverance in prayer. (See Mark 7:25–30.) The case of blind Bartimaeus makes the same point. (See Mark 10:46–52.) Jairus (see Mark 5:22–24, 35–43) and the centurion (see Matthew 8:5–13) illustrate and emphasize other aspects of prayer. The parable of the Pharisee and the tax collector urge humility in prayer, declare the wondrous results of praying, and show the vanity and worthlessness of wrong praying. (See Luke 18:10–14.) The failure to enforce church discipline and the readiness to violate the brotherhood are both used as examples of the far-reaching results of agreeing in prayer. Matthew recorded these words of Jesus:

> *If your brother sins against you, go and tell him his fault between you and him alone. If he hears you, you have gained your brother. But if he will not hear, take with you one or two more, that "by the mouth of two or three witnesses every word may be established." And if he refuses to hear them, tell it to the church. But if he refuses even to hear the church, let him be to you like a heathen and a tax collector. Assuredly, I say to you, whatever you bind on earth will be bound in heaven, and whatever you loose on earth will be loosed in heaven. Again I say to you that if two of you agree on earth concerning anything that they ask, it will be done for them by My Father in heaven. For where two or*

three are gathered together in My name, I
am there in the midst of them.

(Matt. 18:15–20)

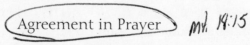 *mk. 19:15*

It is of prayer in concert—two agreed ones, two whose hearts have been keyed into perfect symphony by the Holy Spirit—that Christ is speaking. Anything that they will ask, it will be done. Christ had been speaking of discipline in the church, how things were to be kept in unity, and how the fellowship of the brethren was to be maintained by the restoration of the offender or by his exclusion. Members who had been true to the brotherhood of Christ, and who were laboring to preserve that brotherhood unbroken, would be the ones in agreement to make appeals to God in united prayer.

Prayer Is a Spiritual Directive

In the Sermon on the Mount, Christ lays down constitutional principles. Types and shadows are retired, and the law of spiritual life is declared. In this foundational law of the Christian system, prayer assumes a conspicuous, if not a paramount, position. It is not only wide, all-commanding, and comprehensive in its own sphere of action and relief, but it is also ancillary to all duties. Both the teaching that demands kindly and discriminating judgment toward others, as well as the royal injunction, the Golden Rule of action, owe their being to prayer.

Christ puts prayer among the statutory promises. He does not leave it to natural law. The law of need, of supply and demand, of helplessness, of natural instincts, or the law of sweet, high, attractive privilege—these, however strong as motives of action, are not the basis of praying. Christ puts it as spiritual law. Men must pray. Not to pray is not simply a privation, an omission, but a positive violation of law, of spiritual life, a crime, bringing disorder and ruin. Prayer is law worldwide; it reaches throughout eternity.

The Necessity of Private Prayer

In the Sermon on the Mount many important utterances are dismissed with a line or a verse, while the subject of prayer occupies a large space. Christ returns to it again and again. He bases the possibilities and necessities of prayer on the relationship of father and child, the child crying for bread, and the father giving that for which the child asks. Prayer and its answer are in the relationship of a father to his child. The teaching of Jesus Christ on the nature and necessity of prayer as recorded in His life is remarkable. He sends men to their prayer closets. Prayer must be a holy exercise, untainted by vanity or pride. It must be in secret. The disciple must live in secret. God lives there, is sought there, and is found there. The command of Christ as to prayer is that pride and publicity should be shunned. Prayer is to be in private.

*But you, when you pray, go into your room,
and when you have shut your door, pray to
your Father who is in the secret place; and
your Father who sees in secret will reward
you openly.*   (Matt. 6:6)

Prayer Requires a Right Spirit

The Beatitudes are not only to enrich and
adorn, but they are also the material out of which
spiritual character is built. The very first one of
these fixes prayer in the very foundation of spiritual character, not simply to adorn, but to com-
pose. *"Blessed are the poor in spirit"* (Matt. 5:3).
Again, the word *"poor"* here in the Greek means a
pauper, one who lives by begging. The real Christian lives on the bounties of Another, whose bounties he gets by asking. Prayer then becomes the
basis of Christian character, the Christian's business, his life and his living. This is Christ's law of
prayer, putting it into the very being of the Christian. It is his first step, and his first breath, which
is to color and to form the rest of his life. Blessed
are the poor ones, for only they can pray.

Prayer is the Christian's vital breath,
The Christian's native air;
His watchword at the gates of death,
He enters heaven with prayer.

From praying Christ eliminates all self-
sufficiency and all pride. The poor in spirit are the
praying ones. Beggars are God's princes. They are

God's heirs. Christ removes the rubbish of Jewish traditions and interpretations of the law from the regulations of the prayer altar.

> *You have heard that it was said to those of old, "You shall not murder, and whoever murders will be in danger of the judgment." But I say to you that whoever is angry with his brother without a cause shall be in danger of the judgment. And whoever says to his brother, "Raca!" shall be in danger of the council. But whoever says, "You fool!" shall be in danger of hell fire. Therefore if you bring your gift to the altar, and there remember that your brother has something against you, leave your gift there before the altar, and go your way. First be reconciled to your brother, and then come and offer your gift.* (Matt. 5:21–24)

He who tries to pray to God with an angry spirit, with loose and irreverent lips, with an irreconcilable heart, and with unsettled neighborly scores, spends his labor for what is worse than nothing, violates the law of prayer, and adds to his sin.

How rigidly exacting is Christ's law of prayer. It goes to the heart, and demands that love be enthroned there, love for the brotherhood. The sacrifice of prayer must be seasoned and perfumed with love, by love in the inward parts. The law of prayer, its creator and inspirer, is love.

Praying Brings Results

Praying must be done. God wants it done. He commands it. Man needs it and man must do it. Something must surely come of praying, for God promises that something will come out of it, if men are in earnest and are persevering in prayer.

After Jesus taught, *"Ask, and it will be given to you"* (Matt. 7:7), He encouraged real praying, and more praying. He repeated and asserted with redoubled assurance, *"For everyone who asks receives"* (v. 8). He left no room for exception when He said, *"Everyone." "He who seeks finds"* (v. 8). Here it is again, measured and stamped with infinite truth. It is closed and signed, as well as sealed, with divine attestation: *"To him who knocks it will be opened"* (v. 8).

Note how we are encouraged to pray because of our relationship with God:

> *If you then, being evil, know how to give good gifts to your children, how much more will your Father who is in heaven give good things to those who ask Him!*　　(Matt. 7:11)

Christians Must Pray

The relation of prayer to God's work and God's rule in this world is most fully illustrated by Jesus Christ in both His teaching and His practice. He is first in every way and in everything. Among the rulers of the church He is primary in a preeminent way. He has the throne. The golden crown is His in eminent preciousness. The white garments enrobe Him in incomparable whiteness and beauty. In the ministry of prayer He is a divine example as well as the divine Teacher. His examples and His teaching on prayer abound. How imperative the teaching of our Lord when He affirms that *"men always ought to pray and not lose heart"* (Luke 18:1). Then He presents a striking parable of an unjust judge and a poor widow to illustrate and reinforce His teaching. (See Luke 18:2–8.) It is a necessity to pray. It is exacting and binding for men always to be in prayer. Courage, endurance, and perseverance are demanded so that men may never become discouraged in prayer.

"And shall God not avenge His own elect who cry day and night to Him?" (v. 7). This is His strong and indignant questioning and affirmation. Men must pray according to Christ's teaching. They must not become tired or grow weary in praying. God's character is the assurance that much will come of the persistent praying of true men.

Doubtless the praying of our Lord had much to do with the revelation made to Peter and the confession he made to Christ, *"You are the Christ, the Son of the living God"* (Matt. 16:16). Prayer mightily affects and molds the circle of our associates. Christ made disciples and kept them disciples by praying. His twelve disciples were impressed by His praying. No man ever prayed like He did. How different His praying was from the cold, proud, self-righteous praying that they heard and saw on the streets, in the synagogue, and in the temple.

59

Until now you have asked nothing in My name. Ask, and you will receive, that your joy may be full. —John 16:24

Confess your trespasses to one another, and pray for one another, that you may be healed. The effective, fervent prayer of a righteous man avails much.

—James 5:16

And I will give you the keys of the kingdom of heaven, and whatever you bind on earth will be bound in heaven, and whatever you loose on earth will be loosed in heaven.   —Matthew 16:19

Six

The Lesson of Prayer

Luke tells us that as Jesus was praying in a certain place, when He ceased, one of His disciples said to Him, *"Lord, teach us to pray"* (Luke 11:1). This disciple had heard Jesus preach, but did not feel like saying, "Lord, teach us to preach." He could learn to preach by studying the methods of the Master. But there was something about the praying of Jesus that made the disciple feel that he did not know how to pray, that he had never prayed, and that he could not learn even by listening to the Master as He prayed. There is a profound something about prayer that never lies on the surface. To learn it, one must go to the depths of the soul, and climb to the heights of God.

—A.C. Dixon

L et it not be forgotten that prayer was one of the great truths that Jesus came into the world to teach and illustrate. It was worth a trip from heaven to earth to teach men this great lesson of prayer. It was a great lesson, a very difficult lesson, for men to learn. Men are naturally averse to learning this lesson of prayer. The lesson is a very lowly one. Only God can teach it. It is a despised poverty, a sublime and heavenly vocation. The disciples were very slow-witted students, but were quickened to prayer by hearing Jesus pray and talk about prayer.

The Need to Be Taught

The state of Christ's personality was not and could not be displayed in its fullest and highest sense of need and dependence, yet Christ did try to impress on His disciples not only the deep need for prayer in general, but also the importance of prayer for their personal and spiritual needs. And there were moments when they felt the need of a deeper and more thorough schooling in prayer and of their grave neglect in this regard. One of these hours of deep conviction on their part, as well as of eager inquiry, was when He was praying at a certain place and time, and they saw Him and said to Him, *"Lord, teach us to pray, as John also taught his disciples"* (Luke 11:1).

As they had listened to Him praying, they had felt very keenly their ignorance and deficiency in praying. Who has not felt the same deficiency and ignorance? Who has not longed for a teacher in the divine art of praying?

The conviction that these twelve men had of their shortcomings in prayer arose from hearing their Lord and Master pray, but likewise from their sense of serious deficiency even when they compared their training with John the Baptist's training of his disciples in prayer. As they listened to their Lord pray—for unquestionably He must have been seen and heard by them as He prayed with marvelous simplicity and power, so human and so divine—such praying had a stimulating charm for them. In the presence and hearing of His praying, they felt their ignorance and deficiency in prayer very keenly. Who has not felt the same ignorance and deficiency?

We do not regret the schooling our Lord gave these twelve men, for in schooling them, He schools us. The lesson is one already learned in the law of Christ. But they were so dull that repeated, patient instruction was required to teach them this divine art of prayer. Likewise, we are so dull and inept that many patient repetitions must be taught to us before we will learn any important lesson in the all-important school of prayer.

The Connection between Faith and Prayer

This divine Teacher of prayer lays Himself out to make it clear and strong that God answers prayer, assuredly, certainly, inevitably; that it is the duty of the child to ask and to press; and that the Father is obliged to answer and to give as a result of the asking. In Christ's teaching, prayer is no sterile, vain performance, not a mere rite or a form, but a request for an answer, a plea to gain, the seeking of a great good from God. It is a lesson of getting that for which we ask, of finding that for which we seek, and of entering the door at which we knock (Matt. 7:7; Luke 11:9).

We have a notable example of this as Jesus comes down from the Mount of Transfiguration.

He finds His disciples defeated, humiliated, and confused in the presence of their enemies. A father has brought his child possessed with a demon to have the demon cast out. They tried to do it, but failed. They had been commissioned by Jesus and sent to do that very work, but had signally failed.

> *And when He had come into the house, His disciples asked Him privately, "Why could we not cast it out?" So He said to them, "This kind can come out by nothing but prayer and fasting."* (Mark 9:28–29)

Their faith had not been cultured by prayer. They failed in prayer before they failed in ability to do their work. They failed in faith because they had failed in prayer. The one thing that was necessary to do God's work was prayer. The work that God sends us to do cannot be done without prayer.

In Christ's teaching on prayer we have another pertinent statement. It was in connection with the cursing of the barren fig tree.

> *Jesus answered and said to them, "Assuredly, I say to you, if you have faith and do not doubt, you will not only do what was done to the fig tree, but also if you say to this mountain, 'Be removed and be cast into the sea,' it will be done. And whatever things you ask in prayer, believing, you will receive."* (Matt. 21:21–22)

In this passage we have faith and prayer, their possibilities and powers joined. A fig tree had been blasted to the roots by the words of the Lord Jesus. The power and quickness of the result surprised the disciples. Jesus said to them that it should be no surprise to them that such a difficult work was done. *"If you have faith"* (Matt. 21:21), then faith's possibilities in affecting change will not be confined to the little fig tree, but will also apply to the gigantic, rocky mountains—uprooting and moving them into the sea. Prayer is the leverage behind this great power of faith.

Prayer Secures Workers

It is well to refer again to the occasion when the heart of our Lord was so deeply moved with compassion as He gazed at the multitudes, *"because they were weary and scattered, like sheep having no shepherd"* (Matt. 9:36). Then He urged this injunction upon His disciples, *"Pray the Lord of the harvest to send out laborers into His harvest"* (v. 38), clearly teaching them that it belonged to God to call into the ministry men whom He will call, and that in answer to prayer the Holy Spirit does this very work.

Prayer is as necessary now as it was then to secure the needed laborers to reap earthly harvests for the heavenly granaries. Has the church of God ever learned this lesson of so vital and exacting import? God alone can choose the laborers and thrust them out, and this choosing He does not delegate to man, church, convocation, synod, association, or conference. God is moved by prayer to this great work of calling men into the ministry. Earthly fields are rotting. They are untilled because prayer is silent. The laborers are few. Fields are unworked because prayer to God has not been been exercised.

Abiding in Christ Is Necessary for True Prayer

We have the prayer promise and the prayer ability put in a distinct form in the higher teachings of prayer by our Lord: *"If you abide in Me, and My words abide in you, you will ask what you desire, and it shall be done for you"* (John 15:7).

Here we have a fixed attitude of life as the condition of answered prayer—not simply a fixed attitude of life toward some great principles or purposes, but the fixed attitude and unity of life with Jesus Christ. To live in Him, to dwell there, to be one with Him, to draw all life from Him, to let all life from Him flow through us—this is the attitude of prayer and the ability to pray. No abiding in Him can be separated from His Word abiding in us. It must live in us to give birth to and food for prayer. The attitude of the person of Christ is the condition of prayer.

The Old Testament saints had been taught that God has *"magnified* [His] *word above all* [His] *name"* (Ps. 138:2). New Testament saints must learn fully how to exalt by perfect obedience that Word issuing from the lips of Him who is the Word. Praying ones under Christ must learn what praying ones under Moses had already learned:

"Man shall not live by bread alone, but by every word that proceeds from the mouth of God" (Matt. 4:4). The life of Christ flowing through us and the words of Christ living in us give potency to prayer. They breathe the spirit of prayer, and make the body, blood, and bones of prayer. Then it is Christ praying in me and through me, and all things that I will are the will of God. My will becomes the law and the answer, for it is written, *"You will ask what you desire, and it shall be done for you"* (John 15:7).

Fruit-Bearing Is a Condition of Prayer

Our Lord puts fruit-bearing at the forefront of our praying:

> *You did not choose Me, but I chose you and appointed you that you should go and bear fruit, and that your fruit should remain, that whatever you ask the Father in My name He may give you.* (John 15:16)

Barrenness cannot pray, but fruit bearing capacity and reality can pray. Jesus does not talk about fruitfulness in the past but in the present. He says, *"That your fruit should remain."* Fruit, the product of life, is a condition of praying. A life vigorous enough to bear fruit, much fruit, is the condition and the source of prayer.

> *And in that day you will ask Me nothing. Most assuredly, I say to you, whatever you*

67

ask the Father in My name He will give you. Until now you have asked nothing in My name. Ask, and you will receive, that your joy may be full. (John 16:23–24)

"In that day you will ask Me nothing." Our business is not about solving riddles, revealing mysteries, or curious questionings. This is not our attitude, not our business under the dispensation of the Spirit; instead, we are to pray, and to pray largely. Much true praying increases man's joy and God's glory.

Ask in His Name

"Whatever you ask the Father in My name [I] *will give you,"* says Christ, and the Father will give. Both Father and Son are pledged to give the very things for which we ask. But the condition is *"in* [His] *name."* This does not mean that His name is a talisman to ward off evil and bring good. It does not mean that His name in beautiful settings of pearl will give value to prayer. It is not that His name perfumed with sentiment and mixed with our prayers and actions will do the deed. How fearful the statement,

Many will say to Me in that day, "Lord, Lord, have we not prophesied in Your name, cast out demons in Your name, and done many wonders in Your name?" And then I will declare to them, "I never knew you; depart from Me, you who practice lawlessness!" (Matt. 7:22–23)

How blasting the doom of these great workers and doers who claim to work in His name!

Following Christ means far more than sentiment, verbiage, and nomenclature. It means to stand in His stead, to bear His nature, to stand for all for which He stood: righteousness, truth, holiness, and zeal. It means to be one with God as He was, one in spirit, in will, and in purpose. It means that our praying is singly and solely for God's glory through His Son. It means that we abide in Him, that Christ prays through us, lives in us, and shines out of us; that we pray by the Holy Spirit according to the will of God.

As Christ nears the close of His earthly mission, nearer to the greater and more powerful dispensation of the Spirit, His teaching about prayer takes on a more absorbing and higher form. It has now become a graduate school. His connection with prayer becomes more intimate and more absolute. He becomes in prayer what He is in all else pertaining to salvation, *"the Beginning and the End, the First and the Last"* (Rev. 22:13). His name becomes all potent. Mighty works are to be done by the faith that can pray in His name. Like His nature, His name covers all needs, embraces all worlds, and gets all good.

Do you not believe that I am in the Father, and the Father in Me? The words that I speak to you I do not speak on My own authority; but the Father who dwells in Me does the works. Believe Me that I am in the Father and the Father in Me, or else believe

69

Me for the sake of the works themselves. Most assuredly, I say to you, he who believes in Me, the works that I do he will do also; and greater works than these he will do, because I go to My Father. And whatever you ask in My name, that I will do, that the Father may be glorified in the Son. If you ask anything in My name, I will do it.
(John 14:10–14)

The Father, the Son, and the praying one are all bound up together. All things are in Christ, and all things are in prayer in His name. *"If you ask anything in My name."* The key that unlocks the vast storehouse of God is prayer. The power to do greater works than Christ did lies in the faith that can grasp His name truly and in true praying.

Prayer's Protective Power

At the end of His earthly life, note how He urges prayer as a protection against the many evils to which His disciples were exposed. In view of the temporal and fearful terrors of the destruction of Jerusalem, He charges them to this effect: *"Pray that your flight may not be in winter"* (Matt. 24:20).

How many evils in this life can be escaped by prayer! How many fearful earthly calamities can be mitigated, if not wholly relieved, by prayer! Notice how, amid the excesses and stupefying influences to which we are exposed in this world, Christ charges us to pray:

But take heed to yourselves, lest your hearts be weighed down with carousing, drunkenness, and cares of this life, and that Day come on you unexpectedly. For it will come as a snare on all those who dwell on the face of the whole earth. Watch therefore, and pray always that you may be counted worthy to escape all these things that will come to pass, and to stand before the Son of Man.

(Luke 21:34–36)

Watch and Pray

Even amid the darkness of Gethsemane, with the stupor that had settled upon the disciples, we have the sharp warning from Christ to His sluggish disciples, *"Watch and pray, lest you enter into temptation. The spirit indeed is willing, but the flesh is weak"* (Matt. 26:41). How necessary it is for us to hear such a warning to awaken all our powers, not simply for the great crises of our lives, but as the inseparable and constant attendants of a life marked with perils and dangers on every hand.

In view of the uncertainty of the timing of Christ's coming in judgment, and the uncertainty of the day of our going out of this world, He says:

But of that day and hour no one knows, not even the angels in heaven, nor the Son, but only the Father. Take heed, watch and pray; for you do not know when the time is.

(Mark 13:32)

71

Prayer Equips for Service

We have the words of Jesus as given in His last interview with His twelve disciples, found in the gospel of John, chapters fourteen to seventeen. These are true, solemn parting words. The disciples were to move out into the regions of toil and peril, bereft of the personal presence of their Lord and Master. They were to be impressed that prayer would serve them in everything, and its use and unlimited possibilities would in some measure supply their loss. By it they would be able to command all the possibilities of Jesus Christ and God the Father.

It was the occasion of momentous interest to Jesus Christ. His work was to receive its climax and crown in His death and His resurrection. His glory and the success of His work and its execution under the mastery and direction of the Holy Spirit were to be committed to His apostles. To them it was an hour of strange wonderment and of peculiar, mysterious sorrow. They were only too well assured of the fact that Jesus was to leave them; all else was dark and impalpable.

He was to give them His parting words and pray His parting prayer. Solemn, vital truths were to be the weight and counsel of that hour. He spoke to them of heaven. These young men, strong though they were, could not meet the duties of their preaching life and their apostolic life, without the fact, the thought, the hope, and the relish of heaven. These things were to be present constantly in all sweetness, in all their vigor, in all freshness, and in all brightness. He spoke to them about their spiritual and conscious connection with Himself, an abiding indwelling, so close and continuous that His own life would flow into them, as the life of the vine flows into the branches. (See John 15:1–8.) Their lives and their fruitfulness were dependent upon this connection. Then praying was urged upon them as one of the vital, essential forces. This was the one thing upon which all the divine force depended, and this was the avenue and agency through which the divine life and power were to be secured and continued in their ministry.

He spoke to them about prayer. He had taught them many lessons about this all-important subject as they had been together. He seizes this solemn hour to perfect His teaching. They must be made to realize that they have a limitless and inexhaustible storehouse of good in God, and that they can draw on Him at all times and for all things without limitation. As Paul said in later years to the Philippians, *"My God shall supply all your need according to His riches in glory by Christ Jesus"* (Phil. 4:19).

Having risen a long while before daylight, He went out and departed to a solitary place; and there He prayed.

—Mark 1:35

When you pray, say: Our Father in heaven, hallowed be Your name. Your kingdom come. Your will be done on earth as it is in heaven. Give us day by day our daily bread. And forgive us our sins, for we also forgive everyone who is indebted to us. And do not lead us into temptation, but deliver us from the evil one.

—Luke 11:2–4

Father, if it is Your will, take this cup away from Me; nevertheless not My will, but Yours, be done.

—Luke 22:42

Seven

Jesus, Our Example in Prayer

Christ, when He saw that He must die, and that
now His time was come, wore His body out. He
did not care, as it were, what became of Himself.
He wholly spent Himself in preaching all day, in
praying all night, in preaching in the temple those
terrible parables and praying in the Garden such
prayers as the High Priestly Prayer (John 17) and
"Your will be done" (Matt. 26:42), praying so
earnestly that *"His sweat became like great drops
of blood"* (Luke 22:44).   —Thomas Goodwin

The Bible record of the life of Jesus Christ gives
but a glance at His busy days, a small selection
of His many words, and only a brief record of His
great works. But even in this record we see Him as
being much in prayer. Even though He was busy
and exhausted by the severe strain and toils of His
life, *in the morning, having risen a long while
before daylight, He went out and departed to a solitary place; and there He prayed"* (Mark 1:35).
Alone in the desert and in the darkness with God!

75

To Be like Jesus Is to Pray

Prayer filled the life of our Lord while He was on earth. His life was a constant stream of incense, sweet and perfumed by prayer. When we see how the life of Jesus was but one of prayer, then we must conclude that to be like Jesus is to pray like Jesus and is to live like Jesus. It is a serious life to pray as Jesus prayed.

Jesus' Life Was Marked by Prayer

We cannot follow any chronological order in the praying of Jesus Christ. We do not know what His steps of advance and skill in the divine art of praying were. He is in the act of prayer when we find Him at the fords of the Jordan, when, at the hands of John the Baptist, the waters of baptism are upon Him. Passing over the three years of His ministry, when closing the drama of His life in that terrible baptism of fear, pain, suffering, and shame, we find Him in the spirit, and also in the very act, of praying. The baptism of the Cross, as well as the baptism of the Jordan, are sanctified by prayer. With the breath of prayer in His last sigh, He commits His spirit to God (Luke 23:46). In His first recorded utterances, as well as His first acts, we find Him teaching His disciples how to pray as His first lesson, and as their first duty. (See Luke 11:1–4.) Under the shadow of the Cross, in the urgency and importance of His last interview with His chosen disciples, He is at the same all-important business, teaching the world's teachers how to pray, trying to make prayerful those lips and hearts out of which were to flow the divine deposits of truth (Luke 22:40).

The great eras of His life were created and crowned with prayer. What His habits of prayer during His stay at home and His work as a carpenter in Nazareth were, we have no means of knowing. God has veiled them, and guess and speculation are not only vain and misleading, but also proud and unwholesome. It would be presumptuous searching into what God has hidden, which would make us seek to be wise above that which was written, trying to lift up the veil with which God has covered His own revelation.

We find Christ in the presence of John the Baptist, the famed prophet and preacher. He has left His Nazareth home and His carpenter shop by God's call. He is now at a transitional point. He has moved out to His great work. John's baptism and the baptism of the Holy Spirit are prefatory and are to qualify Him for that work. This epochal and transitional period is marked by prayer.

When all the people were baptized, it came to pass that Jesus also was baptized; and while He prayed, the heaven was opened. And the Holy Spirit descended in bodily form like a dove upon Him, and a voice came from heaven which said, "You are My beloved Son; in You I am well pleased."

(Luke 3:21–22)

This supreme hour in Jesus' history is different from and in striking contrast with, but not in opposition to, His past. The descent and abiding of the Holy Spirit in all His fullness, the opening heavens, and the attesting voice that involved God's recognition of His only Son—all these are the result of, if not the direct creation of and response to, His praying on that occasion.

Imitate Christ in His Spirit of Prayer

"As He was praying" (Luke 11:1), so we are to be praying. If we would pray as Christ prayed, we must be as Christ was, and must live as Christ lived. The character of Christ, the life of Christ, and the spirit of Christ must be ours if we would pray as Christ prayed and would have our prayers answered as He had His prayers answered. The business of Christ even now in heaven at His Father's right hand is to pray for us (Rom. 8:34). Certainly if we are His, if we love Him, if we live for Him, and if we live close to Him, we will catch the contagion of His praying life, both on earth and in heaven. We will learn His trade and carry on His business on earth.

Jesus Christ loved all men, He tasted death for all men, and He intercedes for all men. Let us ask, then, are we the imitators, the representatives, and the executors of Jesus Christ? Then we must in our prayers run parallel with His atonement in its extent. The atoning blood of Jesus Christ gives sanctity and efficiency to our prayers. As worldwide, as broad, and as human as the Man Christ Jesus was, so must be our prayers. The intercessions of Christ's people must give currency and expedition to the work of Christ, carry the atoning blood to its gracious ends, and help to strike off the chains of sin from every ransomed soul. We must be as praying, as tearful, and as compassionate as was Christ.

Prayer Must Be Primary

Prayer affects all things. God blesses the person who prays. He who prays goes out on a long voyage for God and is enriched himself while enriching others, is blessed himself while the world is blessed by his praying. To *"lead a quiet and peaceable life in all godliness and reverence"* (1 Tim. 2:2) is the richest wealth.

The praying of Christ was real. No man prayed as He prayed. Prayer pressed upon Him as a solemn, all-imperative, all-commanding duty, as well as a royal privilege in which all sweetness was condensed, alluring, and absorbing. Prayer was the secret of His power; the law of His life; the inspiration of His work; and the source of His wealth, His joy, His communion, and His strength.

To Christ Jesus prayer occupied no secondary place, but was exacting and paramount, a necessity, a life, the satisfying of a restless yearning, and a preparation for heavy responsibilities.

Closeting with His Father in counsel and fellowship, with vigor and in deep joy—all this was His praying. Present trials, future glory, the history of His church, and the struggles and perils of His disciples in all times and to the very end of time—all these things were born and shaped by His praying.

79

Nothing is more conspicuous in the life of our Lord than prayer. His campaigns were arranged and His victories were gained in the struggles and communion of His all-night praying. By prayer He rent the heavens. Moses and Elijah and the glory of the Transfiguration waited on His praying. His miracles and teaching had their power from the same source. Gethsemane's praying crimsoned Calvary with serenity and glory. His High Priestly Prayer made the history and hastens the triumph of His church on earth. What an inspiration and command to pray is the prayer life of Jesus Christ while he was in this world! What a comment it is on the value, the nature, and the necessity of prayer!

The dispensation of the person of Jesus Christ was a dispensation of prayer. A synopsis of His teaching and practice of prayer was that *men always ought to pray and not lose heart*" (Luke 18:1).

Pray in Jesus' Name

The Jews prayed in the name of their patriarchs and invoked the privileges granted to them by covenant with God. We have a new name and a new covenant, more privileged, more powerful, more comprehensive, more authoritative, and more divine; and as far as the Son of God is lifted above the patriarchs in divinity, glory, and power, by so much should our praying exceed theirs in range of largeness, glory, and power of results.

Jesus Christ prayed to God as Father. Simply and directly, He approached God in the charmed

and revered circle of the Father. The awful, repel-
ling fear was entirely absent, lost in the supreme
confidence of a child.

Jesus Christ crowned His life, His works, and
His teaching with prayer. How His Father attested
to His relationship with Him and put on Him the
glory of answered prayer at His baptism and
transfiguration, when all other glories were
growing dim in the night that was settling on
Him! What almighty power is in prayer when we
are charged and surcharged with but one inspiration and aim! *"Father, glorify Your name"* (John
12:28). This attitude sweetens all, brightens all,
conquers all, and gets all. *"Father, glorify Your
name."* That guiding star will illumine the darkest
night and calm the wildest storm; it will make us
brave and true. It is an imperial principle. It will
make an imperial Christian.

The range and power of prayer, so clearly
shown by Jesus in His life and teaching, reveal the
great purposes of God. They not only show the Son
in the reality and fullness of His humanity, but
also reveal the Father.

Pray As a Child

Christ prayed as a child. The spirit of a child
was found in Him. At the grave of Lazarus, *"Jesus
lifted up His eyes and said, 'Father'"* (John 11:41).
Again we hear Him begin His prayer after this
fashion: *"In that hour Jesus rejoiced in the Spirit
and said, 'I thank You, Father'"* (Luke 10:21). So

also on other occasions we find Him in prayer addressing God as His Father, assuming the attitude of the child asking something of his father. What confidence, simplicity, and guilelessness! What readiness, freeness, and fullness of approach are all involved in the spirit of a child! What confiding trust, what assurance, what tender interest! What profound concern and tender sympathy on the Father's part! What respect deepening into reverence! What loving obedience and grateful emotions glow in the child's heart! What divine fellowship and royal intimacy! What sacred and sweet emotions! All these meet in the hour of prayer when the child of God meets His Father in heaven, and when the Father meets His child! We must live as children if we would ask as children. We must act as children if we would pray as children. The spirit of prayer is born of a childlike spirit.

The profound reverence in this relationship of paternity must forever exclude all lightness, frivolity, and pertness, as well as all undue familiarity. Solemnity and gravity become the hour of prayer. It has been well said:

> The worshipper who invokes God under the name of Father and realizes the gracious and beneficent love of God must at the same time remember and recognize God's glorious majesty, which is neither annulled nor impaired, but rather supremely intensified through His fatherly love. An appeal to God as Father, if not associated with reverence and homage before the Divine Majesty,

would betray a lack of understanding of the character of God.

And, we might add, would show a lack of the attributes of a child.

Patriarchs and prophets knew something of the doctrine of the Fatherhood of God to God's family. They *"all died in faith, not having received the promises, but having seen them afar off were assured of them,* [and] *embraced them"* (Heb. 11:13), even though they did not understand them in all their fullness.

> *And all these, having obtained a good testimony through faith, did not receive the promise, God having provided something better for us, that they should not be made perfect apart from us.* (Heb. 11:39–40)

Pray Earnestly

"Behold, he is praying" (Acts 9:11) was God's statement of wonder and surprise to the timid Ananias in regard to Saul of Tarsus. "Behold, He is praying" applied to Christ has in it far more wonder, mystery, and surprise. He, the Maker of all worlds; the Lord of angels and of men; coequal and coeternal with the everlasting God; *"the brightness of His glory and the express image of His person"* (Heb. 1:3); fresh from His Father's glory and from His Father's throne—"Behold, He is praying." To find Him in a lowly, dependent attitude of prayer, the Suppliant of all suppliants, His richest legacy

and His royal privilege to pray—this is the mystery of all mysteries, the wonder of all wonders.

The writer of Hebrews gave a brief but comprehensive statement regarding the habit of our Lord in prayer:

> *Who, in the days of His flesh, when He had offered up prayers and supplications, with vehement cries and tears to Him who was able to save Him from death, and was heard because of His godly fear.* (Heb. 5:7)

We have in this description of our Lord's praying the outgoing of great spiritual forces. He prayed with *"prayers and supplications."* It was no formal, tentative effort. He was intense, personal, and real. He was a pleader for God's good. He was in great need, and He had to cry with *"vehement cries"* made stronger still by His tears. In agony, the Son of God wrestled. His praying was no playing a mere part. His soul was engaged, and all His powers were taxed. Let us pause and look at Him and learn how to pray in earnest. Let us learn how to win in an agony of prayer what seems to be withheld from us. *"Godly fear"*—what a beautiful phrase that is! It occurs only two other times in the New Testament. (See Hebrews 11:7; 12:28.)

Never Too Busy to Pray

Jesus Christ was always a busy man with His work, but He was never too busy to pray. Divine business filled His heart and His hands, consumed

His time, and exhausted His nerves. But with Him even God's work must not crowd out God's praying. Saving people from sin or suffering must not, even with Christ, be substituted for praying, or lessen in the least the time or the intensity of these holiest of seasons. He filled the day with working for God; He employed the night with praying to God. The work of the day made the prayers of the night a necessity. The praying sanctified and made successful the working. Too busy to pray gives religion a Christian burial; it is true, but kills it nevertheless.

In many cases only the bare fact, yet the important and suggestive fact, is stated that He prayed. In other cases the very words that came out of His heart and fell from His lips are recorded. The man of prayer, by preeminence, was Jesus Christ. The epochs of His life were created by prayer, and all the minor details of His life were inspired, colored, and impregnated by prayer.

The prayer words of Jesus are sacred words. By them God speaks to God, and by them God is revealed, and prayer is illustrated and reinforced. Here is prayer in its purest form and in its mightiest power. It would seem that earth and heaven would open their ears wide to catch the words of His praying who was truest God and truest man, divinest of suppliants, who prayed as no man has ever prayed. His prayers are our inspiration and pattern to pray.

Ask, and it will be given to you; seek, and you will find; knock, and it will be opened to you. For everyone who asks receives, and he who seeks finds, and to him who knocks it will be opened.

—Matthew 7:7–8

Likewise the Spirit also helps in our weaknesses. For we do not know what we should pray for as we ought, but the Spirit Himself makes intercession for us with groanings which cannot be uttered.

—Romans 8:26

Now to Him who is able to do exceedingly abundantly above all that we ask or think, according to the power that works in us, to Him be glory in the church by Christ Jesus to all generations, forever and ever.

—Ephesians 3:20–21

Eight

Insights from Prayers
of Our Lord

There was a great cape at the south of Africa and
so many storms and so much loss of life until it
was called the Cape of Death. One day in 1789 a
bold navigator shoved the prow of his vessel into
the storms that thundered around it and found a
calm sea. He then named it the Cape of Good
Hope. So there is a cape that jutted out from earth
into the sea of eternity called death. All were
afraid of it. All navigators, sooner or later, must
contend with these murky waters. But once upon a
time, nearly two thousand years ago, a brave
Navigator from heaven came and drove the prow
of His frail humanity bark down into the gloomy
waters of this cape and lay under its awful power
for three days. Emerging from it, He found it to be
the door to endless calm and joy, and now we call
it Good Hope.   —John W. Baker

One of Christ's most impassioned and sublime
hymns of prayer and praise is found recorded
by both Matthew and Luke, with a few verbal con-
trasts and some diversity of detail and conditions.
(See Matthew 11:25–30 and Luke 10:21–22.) In

this context, Jesus is reviewing the results of His ministry and remarking upon the feeble responses of man to God's vast outlay of love and mercy. He is rebuking men for their ingratitude to God, and is showing the fearfully destructive results of their indifference, considering their increased opportunities, favors, and responsibilities.

Truth Is Revealed to Babes

In the midst of these charges, denunciations, and woes, the seventy disciples return to report the results of their mission. They are full of exhilaration at their success and show it with no little self-congratulation. The spirit of Jesus is diverted, relieved, and refreshed by their animation, catching somewhat the contagion of their joy, and sharing in their triumph. He rejoices, gives thanks, and prays a prayer wonderful in its brevity, its inspiration, and its revelation.

In that hour Jesus rejoiced in the Spirit and said, "I thank You, Father, Lord of heaven and earth, that You have hidden these things from the wise and prudent and revealed them to babes. Even so, Father, for so it seemed good in Your sight. All things have been delivered to Me by My Father, and no one knows who the Son is except the Father, and who the Father is except the Son, and the one to whom the Son wills to reveal Him."

(Luke 10:21–22)

God's Will Comes First

Christ's life was lived in the image of His Father. He was the *"express image of His person"* (Heb. 1:3). And so, for Christ, the spirit of prayer with Christ was to do God's will. His constant affirmation was that He came to do His Father's will, and not His own will. (See, for example, Matthew 26:39, 42; Luke 11:2; John 5:30.) When the fearful crisis came in His life in Gethsemane, along with all its darkness, direness, and dread, with the crushing weight of man's sins and sorrows pressing down upon Him, His spirit and frame crushed and almost expiring, He cried for relief, yet it was not His will that was to be followed. (See Matthew 26:39.) His cry was only an appeal out of weakness and death for God's relief in God's way. God's will was to be the law and the rule of His relief, if relief came.

Character Influences Praying; Praying Influences Character

So he who follows Christ in prayer must have God's will as his law, his rule, and his inspiration. In all praying, it is the man who prays. Man's life and character flow into the prayer closet. There is a mutual action and reaction. The place of prayer has much to do with making the character, while the character has much to do with making the place of prayer. It is *"the effective, fervent prayer of a righteous man* [that] *avails much"* (James 5:16). It is *"with those who call on the Lord out of a pure*

heart" (2 Tim. 2:22) that we are to associate.
Christ was the greatest of prayers because He was
the holiest of men. His character is the praying
character. His spirit is the life and power of prayer.
The best prayer is not the one who has the greatest
fluency, the most brilliant imagination, the richest
gifts, or the most fiery ardor, but the one who has
absorbed the most of the spirit of Christ.

It is he whose character is the nearest to a fac-
simile of Christ. Christ's prayer recorded in Matthew and Luke sets forth the characters of those
on whom God's power is bestowed and to whom
God's person and will are revealed. Jesus said that
God has *"hidden these things from the wise and
prudent"* (Matt. 11:25)—those, for instance, who
are *"wise"* in their own eyes, scholars, cultured,
philosophers, doctors, rabbis, and those who are
"prudent," who can put things together, have insight, comprehension, and eloquence. God's revelation of Himself and His will cannot be sought
out and understood by reason, intelligence, or
great learning. Great men and great minds are
neither the channels nor the depositories of God's
revelation by virtue of their culture, intelligence,
or wisdom. God's system of redemption and provi-
dence is not to be thought out; it is not open only
to the learned and the wise. Those who follow
their own learning and wisdom have always sadly
and darkly missed God's thoughts and God's ways.

God Reveals Himself to the Childlike

The condition of receiving God's revelation
and of holding God's truth is one of the heart, not

one of the head. The ability to receive and search out is like that of a child, a babe, the synonym of teachability, innocence, and simplicity. These are the conditions on which God reveals Himself to men. The world by wisdom cannot know God. The world by wisdom can never receive or understand God, because God reveals Himself to men's hearts, not to their heads. Only hearts can ever know God, can feel God, can see God, and can read God in His Book of Books. God is not grasped by thought but by feeling. The world receives God by revelation, not by philosophy. It is not apprehension, the mental ability to grasp God, but plasticity, the ability to be molded, that men need. It is not by hard, strong, stern, great reasoning that the world finds God or takes hold of God, but by big, soft, pure hearts. Men do not need light to see God as much as they need hearts to feel God.

Human wisdom, great natural talents, and the culture of the schools, however good they may be, can neither be the repositories nor conservators of God's revealed truth. The tree of knowledge has been the bane of faith, ever trying to reduce revelation to a philosophy and to measure God by man. In its pride, it removes God and puts man into God's truth. To become babes again, on our mother's bosom, quieted, weaned, without clamor or protest, is the only position in which to know God. A calmness on the surface and in the depths of the soul, in which God can mirror His will, His Word, and Himself is the attitude toward Him through which He can reveal Himself, and this attitude is the right attitude of prayer.

Prayer Precedes Ministry

Our Lord taught us the lesson of prayer by putting into practice in His life what He taught by His lips. Here is a simple but important statement, full of meaning:

> *And when He had sent the multitudes away, He went up on the mountain by Himself to pray. Now when evening came, He was alone there.* (Matt. 14:23)

The multitudes had been fed and were dismissed by our Lord. The divine work of healing and teaching must be stayed awhile in order that time, place, and opportunity for prayer might be secured. Prayer is the divinest of all labor, the most important of all ministries. Away from the eager, anxious, seeking multitudes, He went, while the day was still bright, to be alone with God. The multitudes had taxed and exhausted Him. The disciples were being tossed on the sea (vv. 22, 24), but calmness reigned on the mountaintop where our Lord knelt in secret prayer—where prayer rules.

He must be alone in that moment with God. Temptation was in that hour. The multitude had feasted on the five loaves and two fish. Filled with food and excited beyond measure, they had desired to make Him king. *"When Jesus perceived that they were about to come and take Him by force to make Him king, He departed again to the mountain by Himself alone"* (John 6:15). He flees from the temptation to secret prayer, for it is the source of His strength to resist evil. What a refuge was secret prayer even to Him! What a refuge to us from the world's dazzling and deceptive crowns! What safety there is to be alone with God when the world tempts us, allures us, attracts us! The prayers of our Lord were prophetic and illustrative of the great truth that the greatest measure of the Holy Spirit, the attesting voice and opening heavens, is secured only by prayer. This is suggested by Christ's baptism by John the Baptist, when He prayed as He was baptized and immediately the Holy Spirit descended upon Him *"like a dove"* (Luke 3:22). More than prophetic and illustrative was this hour to Him. This critical hour was real and personal, consecrating and qualifying Him for God's highest purposes. Prayer to Him, just as it is to us, was a necessity—an absolute, invariable condition of securing God's fullest, consecrating, and qualifying power. The Holy Spirit came upon Him in fullness of measure and power in the very act of prayer.

Sonship Is Confirmed through Prayer

And so the Holy Spirit comes upon us in fullness of measure and power only in answer to ardent and intense praying. The heavens were opened to Christ, and access and communion established and enlarged, by prayer. Freedom and fullness of access and closeness of communion are secured to us as the heritage of prayer. The voice attesting His Sonship came to Christ in prayer.

The witness of our sonship, clear and indubitable, is secured only by praying. The constant witness of sonship can be retained only by those who *"pray without ceasing"* (1 Thess. 5:17). When the stream of prayer is shallow and arrested, the evidence of our sonship becomes faint and inaudible.

Nine

Learning from the Prayers of Jesus

Sin is so unspeakably awful in its evil that it struck down, as to death and hell, the very Son of God Himself. He had been amazed enough at sin before. He had seen sin making angels of heaven into devils of hell. Death and all its terrors did not much move or disconcert our Lord. No, it was not death. It was sin. It was hellfire in His soul. It was the coal and the oil and the rosin and the juniper and the turpentine of the fire that is not quenched (Mark 9:43–48).   —Alexander Whyte

We note that from the revelation and inspiration of a transporting prayer-hour of Christ, as its natural sequence, there sounds out that gracious, encouraging proclamation for heavyhearted, restless, weary souls of earth. Christ's words have so impressed, arrested, and drawn humanity as they have fallen on the ears of burdened souls. These words have so sweetened and relieved men of their strenuous work and burdens:

Come to Me, all you who labor and are heavy laden, and I will give you rest. Take My yoke upon you and learn from Me, for I am gentle and lowly in heart, and you will find rest for your souls. For My yoke is easy and My burden is light. (Matt. 11:28–30)

Jesus' Confidence in Prayer

At the grave of Lazarus and as preparatory to and as a condition of calling him back to life, we have our Lord calling on His Father in heaven. *"Father, I thank You that You have heard Me. And I know that You always hear Me"* (John 11:41–42). *"Jesus lifted up His eyes"* (v. 41)—how much was in that heavenly look! How much confidence and plea were in that look to heaven! His very look, the lifting of His eyes, carried His whole being heavenward and caused a pause in that world. His look drew attention and help. All heaven was engaged, pledged, and moved when the Son of God looked up from this grave. Oh, for a people with a Christlike eye, heavenlifted and heaven arresting! As it was with Christ, so should we be so perfected in faith, so skilled in praying, that we could lift our eyes to heaven and say with Him, with deepest humility and with commanding confidence, *"Father, I thank You that You have heard Me."*

Jesus' Directive to Pray

Once more we have a very touching, beautiful, and instructive incident in Christ's praying, which is parabolic as well as historical. This time it had to do with infants in their mothers' arms:

> *Then they brought little children to Him, that He might touch them; but the disciples rebuked those who brought them. But when Jesus saw it, He was greatly displeased and said to them, "Let the little children come to Me, and do not forbid them; for of such is the kingdom of God. Assuredly, I say to you, whoever does not receive the kingdom of God as a little child will by no means enter it." And He took them up in His arms, put His hands on them, and blessed them.*
> (Mark 10:13–16)

This was one of the few times when ignorance and unspiritual views aroused His indignation and displeasure. Vital principles were involved. Foundations were being destroyed, and worldly views influencing the actions of the disciples. Their temper and their words in rebuking those who brought their children to Christ were exceedingly wrong. The very principles that He came to illustrate and propagate were being violated.

Christ received the little ones. The big ones must become little ones. The old ones must become young ones before Christ will receive them. Prayer helps the little ones. The cradle must be invested with prayer. We are to pray for our little ones. Children are now to be brought to Jesus Christ by prayer, as He is in heaven and not on earth. They are to be brought to Him early for His blessing, even when they are infants. His blessing descends on these little ones in answer to the prayers of those who bring them. With untiring importunity they are to be brought to Christ in earnest, persevering prayer by their fathers and mothers. Before they themselves know anything about coming of their own accord, parents are to present them to God in prayer, seeking His blessing on their offspring. At the same time, parents should ask for wisdom, for grace, and for divine help to rear their children so that they may come to Christ when they arrive at the years of accountability.

Holy hands and holy praying have much to do with guarding and training young lives and in forming young characters for righteousness and heaven. What simplicity, kindness, spirituality, humility, and meekness, linked with prayerfulness, are in this act of the divine Teacher!

The Personal Aspect in Jesus' Prayers

It was as Jesus was praying that Peter made that wonderful confession of his faith that Jesus was the Son of God. *"And it happened, as He was alone praying, that His disciples joined Him, and He asked them, saying, 'Who do the crowds say that I am?'"* (Luke 9:18). The disciples answered,

> *"Some say John the Baptist, some Elijah, and others Jeremiah or one of the prophets." He said to them, "But who do you say that I am?" Simon Peter answered and said, "You*

*are the Christ, the Son of the living God."
Jesus answered and said to him, "Blessed
are you, Simon Bar-Jonah, for flesh and
blood has not revealed this to you, but My
Father who is in heaven. And I also say to
you that you are Peter, and on this rock I
will build My church, and the gates of Hades
shall not prevail against it. And I will give
you the keys of the kingdom of heaven, and
whatever you bind on earth will be bound in
heaven, and whatever you loose on earth will
be loosed in heaven."* (Matt. 16:14–19)

It was after our Lord had made large promises
to His disciples, appointing to each of them a
kingdom, that they should sit at His table in His
kingdom and sit on thrones judging the twelve
tribes of Israel (Luke 22:29–30), that He gave
these words of warning to Simon Peter, telling
him that He had prayed for him.

*And the Lord said, "Simon, Simon! Indeed,
Satan has asked for you, that he may sift you
as wheat. But I have prayed for you, that
your faith should not fail; and when you
have returned to Me, strengthen your brethren."* (Luke 22:31–32)

Happy Peter, to have the Son of God pray for
him! Unhappy Peter, to be so in the toils of Satan
as to demand so much of Christ's concern! How
intense are the demands upon our prayers for
some specific cases! Prayer must be personal in

order to be to the fullest extent beneficial. Peter drew on Christ's praying more than any other disciple because of his exposure to greater perils. Pray for the most impulsive, the most endangered ones, by name. Our love and their danger give frequency, inspiration, intensity, and personality to praying.

The Power in Jesus' Prayers

We have seen how Christ had to flee from the multitude after the magnificent miracle of feeding the five thousand as they sought to make Him king. Then prayer was His escape and His refuge from this strong worldly temptation. He returned from that night of prayer with strength and calmness, and with a power to perform that other remarkable miracle of walking on the sea.

Even the loaves and fish were sanctified by prayer before He served them to the multitude. *"And when He had taken the five loaves and the two fish, He looked up to heaven, blessed and broke the loaves"* (Mark 6:41). Prayer should sanctify our daily bread and multiply our seed sown.

He looked up to heaven and heaved a sigh when He touched the tongue of the deaf man who had an impediment in his speech. This sigh was similar to that groaning in spirit that He evinced at the grave of Lazarus. *"Then Jesus, again groaning in Himself, came to the tomb"* (John 11:38). Here was the sigh of the Son of God over a human wreck, groaning that sin and hell had such a mastery over man, troubled that such a desolation and

100

ruin were man's sad inheritance. This is a lesson to be constantly learned by us. Here is a fact always to be kept in mind and heart, and that must ever, in some measure, weigh upon the inner spirits of God's children. We who have received the *"firstfruits of the Spirit...groan within ourselves"* (Rom. 8:23) at sin's waste and death, and are filled with longings for the coming of a better day.

Character and Prayer Are Interconnected

Present in all great praying, making and marking it, is the man. It is impossible to separate the praying from the man. The elements of the man are the constituents of his praying. The man flows through his praying. Only the fiery Elijah could do Elijah's fiery praying. We can get holy praying only from a holy man. Holy being can never exist without holy doing. Being is first; doing comes afterward. What we are gives being, force, and inspiration to what we do. Character, that which is graven deeply, indelibly, imperishably within us, colors all we do.

The praying of Christ, then, is not to be separated from the character of Christ. If He prayed more unweariedly, more self-denyingly, more holily, more simply and directly than other men, it was because these elements entered more largely into His character than into that of others.

Prayer Affects the One Who Prays

The Transfiguration marks another epoch in Christ's life, one that was preeminently a prayer epoch. Luke gives an account of this event along with its intention and purpose:

> *Now it came to pass, about eight days after these sayings, that He took Peter, John, and James and went up on the mountain to pray. As He prayed, the appearance of His face was altered, and His robe became white and glistening. And behold, two men talked with Him, who were Moses and Elijah, who appeared in glory and spoke of His decease which He was about to accomplish at Jerusalem.* (Luke 9:28–31)

The selection was made of three of His disciples for an inner circle of associates in prayer. Few have the spiritual tastes or aptitude for this inner circle. Even these three favored ones could scarcely stand the strain of that long night of praying. We know that He went up on that mountain to pray, not to be transfigured. But it was as He prayed that His appearance was altered and His clothing became white and glistening. There is nothing like prayer to change character and whiten conduct. There is nothing like prayer to bring heavenly visitants and to gild with heavenly glory earth's dull and drear mountain. Peter calls it the *"holy mountain"* (2 Pet. 1:18), made so by prayer.

Jesus Was a Man of Prayer

Three times the voice of God bore witness to the presence and person of His Son, Jesus Christ.

First, at His baptism by John the Baptist, and then at His transfiguration, where the approving, consoling, and witnessing voice of His Father was heard. Jesus was found in prayer both of these times. The third time the attesting voice came, it was not on the heights of His transfigured glory, nor was it as He was girding Himself to begin His conflict and to enter upon His ministry, but it was when He was hastening to the awful end. He was entering the dark mystery of His last agony, and looking ahead to it. The shadows were deepening, a dire calamity was approaching, and an unknown and untried dread was before Him. As He pondered His approaching death, prophesying about it, and forecasting the glory that would follow—in the midst of His high and mysterious discourse— the shadows came like a dread eclipse, and He burst out in an agony of prayer.

> *"Now My soul is troubled, and what shall I say? 'Father, save Me from this hour'? But for this purpose I came to this hour. Father, glorify Your name." Then a voice came from heaven, saying, "I have both glorified it and will glorify it again." Therefore the people who stood by and heard it said that it had thundered. Others said, "An angel has spoken to Him." Jesus answered and said, "This voice did not come because of Me, but for your sake."* (John 12:27–30)

But let it be noted that Christ is meeting and illuminating this fateful and distressing hour with

103

prayer. Even then, the flesh reluctantly shrank from the contemplated end!

How fully does His prayer on the cross for His enemies synchronize with all He taught about love to our enemies, and mercy and forgiveness to those who have trespassed against us! *"Then Jesus said, 'Father, forgive them, for they do not know what they do'"* (Luke 23:34). Apologizing for His murderers, and praying for them while they were jeering and mocking Him at His death pains, and their hands were reeking with His blood—what amazing generosity, pity, and love!

Jesus Revealed His Heart in Prayer

Again, take another one of the prayers on the cross. How touching the prayer and how bitter the cup! How dark and desolate the hour as He exclaims, *"My God, My God, why have You forsaken Me?"* (Matt. 27:46). This is the last stroke that tears His heart in two, more exquisite in its bitterness and its anguish and more heart-piercing than the kiss of Judas. All else was looked for, all else was put in His book of sorrows. How excruciating to have His Father's face withdrawn, to be forsaken by His Father during the hour when these distressing words escaped the lips of the dying Son of God! And yet how truthful He is! How childlike we find Him! And so when the end really comes, we hear Him again speaking to His Father: *"'Father, "into Your hands I commit My spirit."' Having said this, He breathed His last"* (Luke 23:46).

Ten

Our Lord's Model Prayer

What satisfaction must it be to learn from God Himself with what words and in what manner He would have us pray to Him so as not to pray in vain! We do not sufficiently consider the value of this prayer, the respect and attention that it requires, the preference to be given to it, its fulness and perfections, the frequent use we should make of it, and the spirit that we should bring with it. *"Lord, teach us* [how] *to pray"* (Luke 11:1).

—Adam Clark

J esus gives us the pattern of prayer in what is commonly known as the Lord's Prayer. In this model, perfect prayer, He gives us a form to be followed, and yet one to be filled in and enlarged as we may decide when we pray. The outlines and form are complete, yet it is but an outline, with many blanks that our needs and convictions are to fill in.

Prayer Needs Words

Christ puts words on our lips, words that are to be uttered by holy lives. Words belong to the life of prayer. Wordless prayers are like human spirits; they may be pure and high, but are too ethereal and intangible for earthly conflicts and earthly needs and uses. We must have spirits clothed in flesh and blood, and our prayers must be likewise clothed in words to give them point and power, a local habitation, and a name.

Prayer Honors God's Name

This lesson of the Lord's Prayer, elicited by the request of the disciples, *"Lord, teach us to pray"* (Luke 11:1), has something in form and verbiage like the prayer sections of the Sermon on the Mount. It is the same great lesson of praying to *"our Father in heaven"* (v. 2), and is one of insistent importunity. No prayer lesson would be complete without it. It belongs to the first and last lessons in prayer. God's Fatherhood gives shape, value, and confidence to all our praying.

Christ teaches us that to hallow God's name is the first and the greatest of prayers. A desire for the coming and the establishment of God's glorious kingdom follows in value and in sequence the hallowing of God's name. He who really hallows God's name will hail the coming of the kingdom of God, and will labor and pray to bring that kingdom to pass and to establish it. Christ's pupils in the school of prayer are to be taught diligently to hallow God's name; to work for God's kingdom; and to do God's will perfectly, completely, and gladly, *"as it is in heaven"* (v. 2).

Prayer Establishes God's Will on Earth

Prayer engages the highest interests and secures the highest glory of God. God's name, God's kingdom, and God's will are all in it. Without prayer His name is profaned, His kingdom fails, and His will is devalued and opposed. God's will can be done on earth as it is done in heaven. God's will done on earth makes earth like heaven. Persevering prayer is the mighty energy that establishes God's will on earth as it is established in heaven.

Prayer Provides Bread, Forgiveness, and Protection from Evil

Christ is still teaching us that prayer sanctifies and makes hopeful and sweet our daily work for daily bread. Forgiveness of sins is to be sought by prayer, and the great prayer plea we are to make for our forgiveness is that we have forgiven all those who have sinned against us (Matt. 6:12). It involves love for our enemies so far as to pray for them, to bless them and not curse them, and to pardon their offences against us whatever those offences may be (Luke 6:27–29).

We are to pray, *"Do not lead us into temptation"* (Matt. 6:13), that is, while we thus pray, the Tempter and the temptation are to be watched against, resisted, and prayed against.

Prayer Is for All Stages of Life

Jesus lays down all these things in this law of prayer, but He teaches many simple lessons through the comments and expressions He adds to expand and explain His model prayer.

In this prayer He teaches His disciples to pray words that have become so familiar to thousands in this day who learned it at their mothers' knees in childhood. These words are so childlike that children find their instruction, edification, and comfort in them as they kneel and pray. The most glowing mystic and the most careful thinker each finds his own language in these simple words of prayer. Beautiful and revered as these words are, they are our words for solace, help, and learning.

Christ led the way in prayer so that we might follow His footsteps. Matchless Leader in matchless praying! Lord, teach us to pray as You Yourself pray!

How marked the contrast is between the High Priestly Prayer and this Lord's Prayer, the model for praying that He gave to His disciples as the first elements of prayer. How simple and childlike! No one has ever approached in composition a prayer so simple in its petitions and yet so comprehensive in all of its requests.

How these simple elements of prayer as given by our Lord commend themselves to us! This prayer is for us as well as for those to whom it was first given. It is for the child in the ABCs of prayer, and it is for the graduate of the highest institutions of learning. It is a personal prayer, reaching to all our needs and covering all our sins. It is the highest form of prayer for others. As the student can never in all his studies or learning dispense with his ABCs, and as the alphabet gives form, color, and expression to everything that is learned after it, impregnating and grounding everything, so the learner in Christ can never dispense with the Lord's Prayer. But he may make it form the basis of his higher praying, such as intercession for others as is seen in Christ's High Priestly Prayer.

The Lord's Prayer becomes ours at our mother's knee and fits us in all the stages of a joyous Christian life. The High Priestly Prayer is ours also in the stages and office of our royal priesthood as intercessors before God. Here we have oneness with God, deep, spiritual unity and unswerving loyalty to God. We live and pray to glorify God.

Pray without ceasing.
                    —1 Thessalonians 5:17

I do not pray for these alone, but also for those who will believe in Me through their word; that they all may be one, as You, Father, are in Me, and I in You; that they also may be one in Us, that the world may believe that You sent Me.   —John 17:20–21

Watch and pray, lest you enter into temptation. The spirit indeed is willing, but the flesh is weak.   —Mark 14:38

Eleven

Our Lord's High Priestly Prayer

Jesus closes His life with inimitable calmness, confidence, and sublimity. *"I have glorified You on the earth. I have finished the work which You have given Me to do"* (John 17:4). The annals of earth have nothing comparable to it in real serenity and sublimity. May we come to our end thus, in supreme loyalty to Christ.　　—E. M. Bounds

We come now to consider our Lord's High Priestly Prayer, as found recorded in the seventeenth chapter of John's gospel. Obedience to the Father and abiding in the Father belong to the Son and belong to us, as partners with Christ in His divine work of intercession. How tenderly, how compassionately, and how fully He prays for His disciples! *"I pray for them. I do not pray for the world"* (John 17:9). What a pattern of prayerfulness for God's people! For God's people are God's cause, God's church, and God's kingdom. Pray for God's people, for their unity, their sanctification, and their glorification. How the subject of their unity pressed upon Him! These walls of separation, these alienations, these fractured circles of

111

God's family, and these warring tribes of ecclesiastics—how He is torn and bleeds and suffers afresh
at the sight of these divisions! Unity—that is the
great burden of the remarkable High Priestly
Prayer. *"That they may be one as We are"* (John
17:11, see also, verse 22). The spiritual oneness of
God's people is the heritage of God's glory to
them, transmitted by Christ to His church.

Jesus Prays for Himself

First of all, in this prayer, Jesus prays for
Himself. He does not petition, as in Gethsemane,
out of weakness, but in strength. Now there is not
the pressure of darkness and hell, but passing for
the time over the fearful interim, He asks that He
may be glorified, and that His exalted glory may
secure glory to His Father. His sublime loyalty and
fidelity to God are declared, that fidelity to God
that is the very essence of prayer. Our devoted
lives pray. Our unswerving loyalty to God are elo-
quent pleas to Him, and give access and confidence
in our advocacy. This prayer is gemmed, but its
walls are unshakable. What profound and granite
truths! What fathomless mysteries! What deep and
rich experiences such statements as these involve:

*And this is eternal life, that they may know
You, the only true God, and Jesus Christ
whom You have sent....And all Mine are
Yours, and Yours are Mine, and I am glorified in them....And I have declared to them
Your name, and will declare it, that the love
with which You loved Me may be in them,*

*and I in them....And now, O Father, glorify
Me together with Yourself, with the glory
which I had with You before the world was.*
                              (John 17:3, 10, 26, 5)

Let us stop and ask, do we have eternal life? Do
we know God experientially, consciously, really,
and personally? Do we know Jesus Christ as a person, and as a personal Savior? Do we know Him by
a heart acquaintance, and know Him well? This,
this only, is eternal life. And is Jesus glorified in
us? Let us continue this personal inquiry. Do our
lives prove His divinity? Does Jesus shine brighter
because of us? Are we opaque or transparent bod-
ies, and do we darken or reflect His pure light?
Once more let us ask: Do we seek God's glory? Do
we seek glory where Christ sought it? *"Glorify Me
together with Yourself"* (John 17:5). Do we esteem
the presence and the possession of God as our
most excellent glory and our supreme good?

How closely does He bind Himself and His Father to His people! His heart centers on them in
this high hour of holy communion with His Father.

*I have manifested Your name to the men
whom You have given Me out of the world.
They were Yours, You gave them to Me, and
they have kept Your word. Now they have
known that all things which You have given
Me are from You. For I have given to them
the words which You have given Me; and
they have received them, and have known*

113

*surely that I came forth from You; and they
have believed that You sent Me. I pray for
them. I do not pray for the world but for
those whom You have given Me, for they are
Yours. And all Mine are Yours, and Yours
are Mine, and I am glorified in them.*

(John 17:6–10)

Jesus Prays for His Followers

He prays also for keeping for His disciples.
Not only were they to be chosen, elected, and possessed, but also kept by the Father's watchful eyes
and by the Father's omnipotent hand.

*Now I am no longer in the world, but these
are in the world, and I come to You. Holy
Father, keep through Your name those
whom You have given Me, that they may be
one as We are.*   (John 17:11)

He prays that they might be kept by the Holy
Father in all holiness by the power of His Name.
He asks that His people may be kept from sin,
from all sin, from sin in the concrete and sin in the
abstract, from sin in all its shapes of evil, from all
sin in this world. He prays that they might not
only be fit and ready for heaven, but also ready
and fit for earth, for its sweetest privileges, its
sternest duties, its deepest sorrows, and its richest
joys. He prays that they might be ready for all of
its trials, consolations, and triumphs. *"I do not
pray that You should take them out of the world,*

114

but that You should keep them from the evil one"
(John 17:15).

He prays that they might be kept from the
world's greatest evil: sin. He desires that they may
be kept from the guilt, the power, the pollution,
and the punishment of sin. He prays that they
might be kept from the Devil, so that he might not
touch them, find them, or have a place in them;
that they all might be owned, possessed, filled, and
guarded by God. *"Kept by the power of God
through faith for salvation"* (1 Pet. 1:5).

Jesus Entrusts His Followers
to the Father's Care

He places us in the arms of His Father, on the
bosom of His Father, and in the heart of His Father. He calls God into service and places us under
His Father's closest keeping, under His Father's
shadow, and under the shelter of His Father's
wing. The Father's rod and staff are for our secu-
rity, our comfort, our refuge, our strength, and
our guidance.

These disciples were not to be taken out of the
world, but kept from its evil, its monstrous evil,
which is itself. *"Deliver us from this present evil
age"* (Gal. 1:4). How the world seduces, dazzles,
and deludes the children of men! His disciples are
chosen out of the world, out of the world's bustle
and worldliness, out of its all-devouring greed of
gain, out of its money-desire, money-love, and
money-toil. Earth draws and holds as if it were

made out of gold and not out of dirt, as though it were covered with diamonds and not with graves.

"They are not of the world, just as I am not of the world" (John 17:14). They were to be kept not only from sin and Satan, but also from the soil, stain, and the taint of worldliness, as Christ was free from it. Their relationship to Christ was to free them from the world's defiling taint, its unhallowed love, and its criminal friendships. The world's hatred would inevitably follow their Christlikeness. No result so necessarily and universally follows its cause as this: *"The world has hated them because they are not of the world, just as I am not of the world"* (v. 14).

How solemn and almost terrifying the repetition of the declaration, *"They are not of the world, just as I am not of the world"* (v. 16). How pronounced, radical, and eternal was our Lord Christ's divorce from the world! How pronounced, radical, and eternal is our Lord's true followers' separation from the world! The world hates the disciples as it hated their Lord, and will crucify the disciples just as it crucified their Lord. How pertinent are these questions: Are we Christlike in our detachment from this world? Does the world hate us as it hated our Lord? Are His words fulfilled in us?

> *If the world hates you, you know that it hated Me before it hated you. If you were of the world, the world would love its own. Yet because you are not of the world, but I chose you out of the world, therefore the world hates you.* (John 15:18–19)

He presents Himself to us as a true portrait of an unworldly Christian. Here is our changeless pattern. *"They are not of the world, just as I am not of the world"* (John 17:14, 16). We must be modeled after this pattern.

Jesus Prays for Unity

The subject of His followers' unity pressed upon Him. Note how He called His Father's attention to it, and see how He pleaded for their unity:

> *Now I am no longer in the world, but these are in the world, and I come to You. Holy Father, keep through Your name those whom You have given Me, that they may be one as We are.* (John 17:11)

Again He returns to this subject as He foresees the great crowds flocking to His standard as the ages pass on:

> *That they all may be one, as You, Father, are in Me, and I in You; that they also may be one in Us, that the world may believe that You sent Me. And the glory which You gave Me I have given them, that they may be one just as We are one: I in them, and You in Me; that they may be made perfect in one, and that the world may know that You have sent Me, and have loved them as You have loved Me.* (John 17:21–23)

117

Notice how intently His heart was set on this unity. What shameful and bloody history has this lack of unity written for God's church! These walls of separations, these alienations, these divided circles of God's family, these warring tribes of men, and these deadly battles among brothers! Christ looks ahead and sees how He is torn, how He bleeds and suffers afresh in all these sad events of the future. The unity of God's people was to be the heritage of God's glory promised to them. Division and strife are the Devil's bequest to the church, a heritage of failure, weakness, shame, and woe.

The oneness of God's people was to be the one credential to the world of the divine nature of Christ's mission on earth. Let us ask in all candor, Are we praying for this unity as Christ prayed for it? Are we seeking the peace, the welfare, the glory, the might, and the divine nature of God's cause as it is found in the unity of God's people?

Note how He puts Himself as the champion and the pattern of this unworldliness that He prays may possess His disciples. He sends them into the world just as His Father sent Him into the world. He expects them to be and do just as He was and as He did for His Father. He sought the sanctification of His disciples so that they might be wholly devoted to God and purified from all sin. He desired in them a holy life and a holy work for God. He devoted Himself to death in order that they might be devoted in life to God. He prayed For a true sanctification, a real, whole, and thorough sanctification, embracing soul, body, and mind, for time and eternity. With Him the Word itself had much to do with their true sanctification. *"Sanctify them by Your truth. Your word is truth....And for their sakes I sanctify Myself, that they also may be sanctified by the truth"* (John 17:17, 19).

Entire devotedness was to be the type of their sanctification. His prayer for their sanctification marks the pathway to full sanctification. Prayer is that pathway. All the ascending steps to that lofty position of entire sanctification are steps of prayer, increasing prayerfulness in spirit and increasing prayerfulness in fact. *"Pray without ceasing"* (1 Thess. 5:17) is the imperative prelude to *"May the God of peace Himself sanctify you completely"* (v. 23). And prayer is but the continued interlude and doxology of this rich grace in the heart: *"May your whole spirit, soul, and body be preserved blameless at the coming of our Lord Jesus Christ. He who calls you is faithful, who also will do it"* (vv. 23–24).

We can only meet our full responsibilities and fulfill our high mission when we go forth sanctified as Christ our Lord was sanctified. He sends us into the world just as His Father sent Him into the world. He expects us to be as He was, to do as He did, and to glorify the Father just as He glorified the Father. What longings He had to have us with Him in heaven: *"Father, I desire that they also whom You gave Me may be with Me where I am, that they may behold My glory which You have given Me"* (John 17:24). What response do our truant hearts make to this earliest, loving longing of Christ? Are we as eager for heaven as He is to have us there? How calm, how majestic, and how authoritative is His *"I desire."*

He closes His life with inimitable calmness, confidence, and sublimity. *"I have glorified You on the earth. I have finished the work which You have given Me to do"* (John 17:4).

The annals of earth have nothing comparable to it in real serenity and sublimity. May we come to our end thus in supreme loyalty to Christ.

Twelve

The Gethsemane Prayer

The cup, the cup, the cup! Our Lord did not use many words, but He used His few words again and again—*"this cup"* and *"Your will"* (Luke 22:42). *"Your will be done"* (Matt. 26:42), and *"Let this cup pass"* (v. 39) were His prayer. "The cup, the cup, the cup!" cried Christ—first on His feet, then on His knees, and then on His face. *"Lord, teach us to pray"* (Luke 11:1).

—Alexander Whyte

We come to Gethsemane. What a contrast to His High Priestly Prayer, which was a prayer of intense feelings, of universal grasp, and of worldwide and infinite sympathy and concern for His church. Perfect calmness and perfect poise reigned in His High Priestly Prayer. He was majestic, simple, and free from passion or disquiet. As royal Intercessor and Advocate for others, His petitions were like princely edicts, judicial and authoritative. How changed now! In Gethsemane He seems to have entered another region and become another man. His Priestly Prayer, so exquisite in its tranquil flow, so unruffled in its strong, deep current, is like the sun, moving in its orbit with unsullied glory as it brightens, vitalizes, ennobles, and blesses everything. The Gethsemane Prayer is that same sun declining in the West, plunged into an ocean of storm and cloud, storm-covered, storm-eclipsed, with gloom, darkness, and terror on every side.

Jesus Prayed with Great Sorrow

The prayer in Gethsemane is exceptional in every way. The oppressive load of the world's sin is upon Him. The lowest point of His depression has been reached. The bitterest cup of all, His bitter cup, is being pressed to His lips. The weakness of all His weaknesses, the sorrow of all His sorrows, the agony of all His agonies are now upon Him. The flesh is giving out with its fainting and trembling pulsations, like the trickling of His heart's blood. His enemies have thus far triumphed. Hell is in a jubilee, and bad men are joining in the hellish carnival.

Gethsemane was Satan's hour, Satan's power, and Satan's darkness. It was the hour of massing all of Satan's forces for a final, last conflict. Jesus had said, *"The ruler of this world is coming, and he has nothing in Me"* (John 14:30). The conflict for earth's mastery is before Him. The Spirit led and drove Him into the stern conflict and severe temptation of the wilderness. But His Comforter, His leadership, His inspiration through His matchless history seems to have left Him now. *"He began to be sorrowful and deeply distressed"* (Matt. 26:37), and we hear Him under this great pressure exclaiming, *"My soul is exceedingly sorrowful, even to death"* (v. 38). The depression, conflict, and agony had gone to the very core of His spirit, and had sunk Him to the very verge of death. He was *"deeply distressed."*

Surprise and awe depressed His soul. *"Deeply distressed"* was the hour of hell's midnight that fell upon His spirit. He was *"exceedingly sorrowful"* this hour when the sins of all the world, of every man, of all men, with all their stain and all their guilt, fell upon His immaculate soul.

He cannot abide the presence of His chosen friends. They cannot enter into the depths and demands of this fearful hour. His trusted and set watchers are asleep. His Father's face is hidden. His Father's approving voice is silent. The Holy Spirit, who had been with Him in all the trying hours of His life, seems to have withdrawn from the scene. Alone He must drink the cup, alone He must tread the winepress of God's fierce wrath and of Satan's power and darkness, and of man's envy, cruelty, and vindictiveness. The scene is well described by Luke:

> *Coming out, He went to the Mount of Olives, as He was accustomed, and His disciples also followed Him. When He came to the place, He said to them, "Pray that you may not enter into temptation." And He was withdrawn from them about a stone's throw, and He knelt down and prayed, saying, "Father,*

if it is Your will, take this cup away from Me; nevertheless not My will, but Yours, be done." Then an angel appeared to Him from heaven, strengthening Him. And being in agony, He prayed more earnestly. Then His sweat became like great drops of blood falling down to the ground. When He rose up from prayer, and had come to His disciples, He found them sleeping from sorrow. Then He said to them, "Why do you sleep? Rise and pray, lest you enter into temptation."

(Luke 22:39–46)

Jesus Prayed for Relief

The prayer agony of Gethsemane crowns Calvary with glory, and while the prayers offered by Christ on the cross are the union of weakness and strength, of deepest agony and desolation, here they are accompanied by sweetest calm, divine submission, and implicit confidence.

Nowhere in prophet or priest, king or ruler, synagogue or church, does the ministry of prayer assume such marvels of variety, power, and fragrance as in the life of Jesus Christ. It is the aroma of God's sweetest spices, aflame with God's glory and consumed by God's will.

We find in this Gethsemane Prayer what we find nowhere else in the praying of Christ. *"O My Father, if it is possible, let this cup pass from Me; nevertheless, not as I will, but as You will"* (Matt. 26:39). This is different from the whole tenor and trend of His praying and doing. How different from His High Priestly Prayer! *"Father, I desire"* (John 17:24) is the law and life of that prayer. In His last directions for prayer, He makes our will the measure and condition of prayer. *"If you abide in Me, and My words abide in you, you will ask what you desire, and it shall be done for you"* (John 15:7). He said to the Syro-Phoenician woman, *"Great is your faith! Let it be to you as you desire"* (Matt. 15:28).

But in Gethsemane His praying was against the declared will of God. The pressure was so heavy upon Him, the cup was so bitter, the burden was so strange and intolerable, that the flesh cried out for relief. Prostrate, sinking, *"exceedingly sorrowful, even to death"* (Mark 14:34), He sought to be relieved from what seemed too heavy to bear. He prayed, however, not in revolt against God's will, but in submission to that will, and yet He prayed to change God's plan and to alter God's purposes. Pressed by the weakness of the flesh and by the powers of hell in all their dire, hellish malignity and might, Jesus was on this single occasion constrained to pray against the will of God. He did it, though, with great wariness and pious caution. He did it with declared and inviolable submission to God's will. But this was exceptional.

Conformity Is More Than Submission

Simple submission to God's will is not the highest attitude of the soul to God. Submission may be seeming, induced by conditions, nothing but an enforced surrender, not cheerful but grudging, only a temporary convenience, an intermittent resolve. When the occasion or calamity that called it forth is removed, the will returns to its old ways and to its old self.

With this one exception, Jesus Christ always prayed in conformity with the will of God. He was one with God's plan, one with God's will. To pray in conformity with God's will was the life and law of Christ. Conformity, to live in oneness with God, is a far higher and diviner life than to live simply in submission to God. To pray in conformity—together with God—is a far higher and diviner way to pray than mere submission. At its best state, submission is non-rebellion, an acquiescence, which is good, but not the highest. The most powerful form of praying is positive, aggressive, mightily outgoing and creative. It molds things, changes things, and brings things to pass.

Conformity means to *"stand perfect and complete in all the will of God"* (Col. 4:12). It means to delight to do God's will, to run with eagerness and ardor to carry out His plans. Conformity to God's will involves submission—patient, loving, sweet submission. But submission in itself falls short of and does not include conformity. We may be submissive but not conformed. We may accept results against which we have warred, and even be resigned to them.

Conformity means to be one with God, both in result and in processes. Submission may be one with God in the end. Conformity is one with God

in the beginning and the end. Jesus had conformity, absolute and perfect, to God's will, and by
that He prayed. This was the single point where
there was a drawing back from God's processes,
extorted by insupportable pain, fear, and weari-
ness. His submission was abject, loyal, and confiding, as His conformity had been constant and
perfect. Conformity is the only true submission,
the most loyal, the sweetest, and the fullest.

Suffering Yields to Perfection

Gethsemane has its lessons of humble supplications, as Jesus knelt alone in the Garden; lessons of burdened prostration, as He fell on His
face; of intense agony; of distressing dread; of
hesitancy and shrinking back; of crying out for relief—yet amid it all, of cordial submission to God,
accompanied with a singleness of purpose for His
glory.

Satan will have for each of us his hour and
power of darkness (see Luke 22:53) and for each of
us the bitter cup and the fearful spirit of gloom.

We can act against God's will as Moses did
when he struck the rock and was denied entrance
to the Promised Land (see Numbers 20:2–12), or
pray against God's will as Paul did three times
about the thorn in the flesh (see 2 Corinthians
12:7–9); as David did for his doomed child (see 2
Samuel 12:15–23); as Hezekiah did to live (see 2
Kings 20:1–19). We may pray against God's will
three times when the stroke is the heaviest, the

sorrow is the keenest, and the grief is the deepest. We may lie prostrate all night, as David did, through the hours of darkness. We may pray for hours, as Jesus did, and in the darkness of many nights, not measuring the hours by the clock or the nights by the calendar. It must all be, however, the prayer of submission.

When the sorrow and desolation of Gethsemane fall in heaviest gloom upon us, we ought to submit patiently and tearfully, if need be, but sweetly and resignedly, without tremor or doubt, to the cup pressed by a Father's hand to our lips. *"Not My will, but Yours, be done"* (Luke 22:42), our broken hearts will say. In God's own way, mysterious to us, that cup has in its bitterest dregs, as it had for Christ, the gem and gold of perfection. We are to be put into the crucible to be refined. Christ was made perfect in Gethsemane, not by the prayer, but by the suffering. *"For it was fitting for Him...to make the captain of their salvation perfect through sufferings"* (Heb. 2:10). The cup could not pass because the suffering had to go on and yield its fruit of perfection. Through many hours of darkness and of hell's power, through many sore conflicts with the prince of this world, by drinking many bitter cups, we are to be made perfect. To cry out against the fearful and searching flame of the crucible of the Father's painful processes is natural and is no sin, if there is perfect acquiescence in the answer to our prayer, perfect submission to God's will, and perfect devotion to His glory.

The Highest Praying Overcomes Obstacles
to Prayer

If our hearts are true to God, we may plead with Him about His way and seek relief from His painful processes. But the fierce fire of the crucible and the agonizing victim with His agonizing and submissive prayer is not the normal and highest form of majestic and all-commanding prayer. We can cry out in the crucible and can cry out against the flame that purifies and perfects us. God allows this, hears this, and answers this, not by taking us out of the crucible or by mitigating the fierceness of the flame, but by sending more than an angel to strengthen us. And yet crying out thus, with full submission, does not satisfy the real, high, world-wide, royal, and eternity-reaching urgent requests of prayer.

The prayer of submission must not be used so as to impair or substitute for the higher and mightier prayer of faith. Nor must it be stressed so as to break down importunate and prevailing prayer, which would be to disarm prayer of its efficiency and discrown its glorious results, and would be to encourage listless, sentimental, and feeble praying.

We are ever ready to excuse our lack of earnest and arduous praying, by an imagined and delusive view of submission. We often end praying just where we ought to begin. We quit praying when God waits and is waiting for us to really pray. We are deterred by obstacles from praying, or we succumb to difficulties, and call it submission to God's will. A world of beggarly faith, spiritual laziness, and halfheartedness in prayer is covered under the high and pious name of submission. To have no plan but to seek God's plan and carry it out is the essence and inspiration of Christlike praying. This is far more than putting in a clause of submission. Jesus did this once in seeking to change the purpose of God, but all His other praying was the output of being perfectly at one with the plans and purposes of God. It is after this order that we pray when we abide in Him and when His word abides in us. Then we ask what we will and it is done (John 15:7). It is then that our prayers fashion and create things. Our wills then become God's will and His will becomes ours. The two become one, and there is not a note of discord.

> *Now this is the confidence that we have in Him, that if we ask anything according to His will, He hears us. And if we know that He hears us, whatever we ask, we know that we have the petitions that we have asked of Him.* (1 John 5:14–15)

And then it proves true that *"whatever we ask we receive from Him, because we keep His commandments and do those things that are pleasing in His sight"* (1 John 3:22).

What restraint, forbearance, self-denial, and loyalty to duty to God, and what deference to the Old Testament Scriptures, are in this statement of our Lord:

Do you think that I cannot now pray to My Father, and He will provide Me with more than twelve legions of angels? How then could the Scriptures be fulfilled, that it must happen thus? (Matt. 26:53)

I say to you who hear: Love your enemies, do good to those who hate you,
bless those who curse you, and pray for
those who spitefully use you.
                          —Luke 6:27–28

The harvest truly is great, but the laborers are few; therefore pray the Lord of
the harvest to send out laborers into His
harvest.   —Luke 10:2

Watch therefore, and pray always that
you may be counted worthy to escape
all these things that will come to pass,
and to stand before the Son of Man.
                          —Luke 21:36

Thirteen

The Holy Spirit and Prayer

During the great Welsh Revival a minister was said to be very successful in winning souls. By one sermon that he preached, hundreds were converted. Far away in a valley news reached a brother minister of the marvelous success of this sermon. He desired to find out the secret of the man's great success. He walked the long way and came to the minister's poor cottage, and the first thing he said was, "Brother, where did you get that sermon?" He was taken into a poorly furnished room, and the minister pointed to a spot where the carpet was worn threadbare, near a window that looked out upon the everlasting hills and solemn mountains, and said, "Brother, there is where I got that sermon. My heart was heavy for men. One night I knelt there—and cried for power as I never preached before. The hours passed until midnight struck, and the stars looked down on a sleeping world, but the answer did not come. I prayed on until I saw a faint streak of gray shoot up, then it was silver—silver became purple and gold. Then the sermon came and the power came and men fell under the influence of the Holy Spirit."

—G. H. Morgan

The Gospel without the Holy Spirit would be vain and inconsequential. The gift of the Holy Spirit was vital to the work of Jesus Christ in the Atonement. As Jesus did not begin His work on earth until He was anointed by the Holy Spirit, so the same Holy Spirit is necessary to carry forward and make effective the atoning work of the Son of God. As His anointing by the Holy Spirit at His baptism was an era in His life, so also is the coming of the Holy Spirit at Pentecost a great era in the work of redemption in making effective the work of Christ's church.

The Holy Spirit Brings Divine Help

The Holy Spirit is not only the bright lamp of the Christian era, its Teacher and Guide, but also the divine Helper.

He is the enabling Agent in God's new dispensation of doing. As the pilot takes his stand at the wheel to guide the vessel, so the Holy Spirit takes up His abode in the heart to guide and empower all its efforts. The Holy Spirit executes the whole Gospel through the man by His presence and control of the spirit of the man.

In the execution of the atoning work of Jesus Christ, in its general and more comprehensive operation, or in its minute and personal application, the Holy Spirit is the one efficient Agent, absolute and indispensable.

The Gospel cannot be executed except by the Holy Spirit. He only has the regal authority to do this royal work. Intellect cannot execute it, neither can learning, eloquence, nor truth; not even the revealed truth can execute the Gospel. The marvelous facts of Christ's life told by hearts unanointed by the Holy Spirit will be dry and sterile, or like a "tale told by an idiot, full of sound and fury, signifying nothing" (*Macbeth*, 5.5.26–28). Not even the precious blood can execute the Gospel. Not any, or all of these, though spoken with angelic wisdom and angelic eloquence can execute the Gospel with saving power. Only tongues set on fire by the Holy Spirit can witness to the saving power of Christ with power to save others.

No one dared move about Jerusalem to proclaim the message to the dying multitudes until the Holy Spirit came in baptismal power. John could not utter a word, though he had pillowed his head on Christ's bosom and caught the pulsations of Christ's heart, and though his brain was full of the wondrous facts of that life and of the wondrous words that fell from His lips. John had to wait until a fuller and richer endowment than all of these came on him. Moreover, though she had nurtured Christ and stored her heart and mind full of holy and motherly memories, even Mary needed to be empowered by the Holy Spirit.

The Holy Spirit Comes through Prayer

The coming of the Holy Spirit is dependent upon prayer, for only prayer can surround, with its authority and demands, the realm where this person of the Godhead has His abode. With Christ, it is, ever has been, and ever will be, *"Ask, and it will be given to you; seek, and you will find; knock, and it will be opened to you"* (Matt. 7:7; Luke 11:9). To His disconsolate disciples, He said, *"I will pray the Father, and He will give you another Helper"* (John 14:16). This law of prayer for the Holy Spirit presses on the disciples and on the Master as well, for even Christ was subject to this law. Of so many of God's children it may truly be said, *"You do not have because you do not ask"* (James 4:2). And of many others it might be said, "You have Him in weak measure because you pray for Him in weak measure."

The Holy Spirit is the spirit of all grace and of each grace as well. Purity, power, holiness, faith, love, joy, and all grace are brought into being and perfected by Him. Would we grow in grace in particular? Would we be perfect in all graces? We must seek the Holy Spirit by prayer.

I urge the seeking of the Holy Spirit. We need Him, and we need to stir ourselves up to seek Him. The measure we receive of Him will be gauged by the fervor of faith and prayer with which we seek Him. Our ability to work for God, to pray to God, to live for God, and to affect others for God will be dependent on the measure of the Holy Spirit received by us, dwelling in us, and working through us.

The Holy Spirit Brings Conviction

Christ lays down the clear and explicit law of prayer in this regard for all of God's children. The world needs the Holy Spirit to convict it *"of sin, and of righteousness, and judgment"* (John 16:8), and to make it feel its guiltiness in God's sight. And this spirit of conviction on sinners comes in answer to the prayers of God's people. Moreover, God's children need Him more and more, need His life, His more abundant life, His superabundant life. But that life begins and ever increases as the child of God prays for the Holy Spirit.

> *If you then, being evil, know how to give good gifts to your children, how much more will your heavenly Father give the Holy Spirit to those who ask Him!* (Luke 11:13)

This is the law, a condition brightened by a promise and sweetened by a relationship.

The Holy Spirit Must Be Sought

The gift of the Holy Spirit is one of the benefits flowing to us from the glorious presence of Christ at the right hand of God; and this gift of the Holy Spirit, together with all the other gifts of the enthroned Christ, are secured to us by prayer. The Bible by express statement, as well as by its general principles and clear and constant intimations, teaches us that the gift of the Holy Spirit is connected with and conditional on prayer. That the Holy Spirit is in the world as God is in the world is true. That the Holy Spirit is in the world as Christ is in the world is also true. It is additionally true that there is nothing declared of Him being in us and in the world that is not declared of God and Christ being in us and in the world. The Holy Spirit was in the world in a measure before Pentecost, and in the measure of His operation then, He was prayed for and sought for, and the principles are unchanged. The truth is, if we cannot pray for the Holy Spirit, we cannot pray for any good thing from God, for He is the sum of all good to us. We seek after the Holy Spirit just as we seek after God, and just as we seek after Christ, with strong cries and tears, and we are to seek always for more and more of His gifts, power, and grace. The presence and power of the Holy Spirit at any given meeting is conditional on praying faith.

Christ lays down the doctrine that the reception of the Holy Spirit is conditional on prayer, and He Himself illustrated this universal law, for when the Holy Spirit came upon Him at His baptism, He was praying. The apostolic church in action illustrated the same great truth.

A few days after Pentecost the disciples were in an agony of prayer. *"And when they had prayed, the place where they were assembled together was shaken; and they were all filled with the Holy Spirit"* (Acts 4:31). This incident destroys every theory that denies prayer as the condition of the coming and re-coming of the Holy Spirit after Pentecost; it confirms the view that the pouring out of the Spirit at Pentecost as the result of a long struggle of prayer illustrates and affirms that God's great and most precious gifts are conditional on asking, seeking, knocking, and praying ardently and persistently.

The same truth comes to the front very prominently in Philip's revival at Samaria. Though filled with joy by believing in Christ, and though received into the church by water baptism, the new believers did not receive the Holy Spirit until Peter and John went down there and prayed with and for them. (See Acts 8:5–17.)

Paul's praying was God's proof to Ananias that Paul was in a state that conditioned him to receive the Holy Spirit. (See Acts 9:10–18.)

The Holy Spirit Empowers Prayer

The Holy Spirit is our Teacher, our Inspirer, and our Revealer in prayer. The power of our praying in degree and force is measured by the Spirit's power working in us, as the will and work of God, according to God's *"good pleasure"* (Phil. 2:13). In the third chapter of Ephesians, after the marvelous prayer of Paul for the church, he seemed to be apprehensive that the Ephesians would think he had gone beyond the ability of God in his large asking. And so he closed his appeal for them with the words, "[God] *is able to do exceedingly abundantly above all that we ask or think"* (Eph. 3:20). The power of God to act for us is measured by the power of God in us. *"According to,"* said the Apostle to the Gentiles, that is, after the measure of, *"the power that works in us"* (v. 20). The effectiveness of our prayers is directly related to the effective working of God in us. A feeble operation of God in us brings feeble praying. The mightiest operation of God in us brings the mightiest praying. The secret of prayerlessness is the absence of the work of the Holy Spirit in us. The secret of feeble praying wherever it occurs is the lack of God's Spirit in His mightiness.

The ability of God to answer and work through our prayers is measured by the divine energy that God has been enabled to put in us by the Holy Spirit. The effectiveness of our praying is the measure of the Holy Spirit in us. The statement of James speaks to this effect: *"The effective, fervent prayer of a righteous man avails much"* (James 5:16). The prayer forged in the heart by the almighty energy of the Holy Spirit works mightily in its results just as Elijah's prayer did (vv. 17–18).

Would we pray efficiently and mightily? Then the Holy Spirit must work in us efficiently and mightily. Paul made the principle of universal application. *"To this end I also labor, striving according to His working which works in me mightily"* (Col. 1:29). All labor for Christ that does not spring from the Holy Spirit working in us is inconsequential and vain. Our prayers and activities are so feeble and lacking in results because He has not worked in us His glorious work. Would you pray with mighty results? Seek the mighty workings of the Holy Spirit in your own spirit.

The Holy Spirit Is a Gift

We have the initial lesson in prayer for the gift of the Holy Spirit, which was to enlarge to its full harvest in Pentecost. In John 14:16, Jesus promises to ask the Father to send another Comforter who will dwell with His disciples and be in them. Note that this is not a prayer that the Holy Spirit might do His work in making us children of God by regeneration, but for that fuller grace and power and person of the Holy Spirit that we can claim by virtue of our relationship to God as His children. His work in us to *make* us the children of God, and His person abiding with us and in us, as children of God, are entirely different stages of the same Spirit's relationship to us. In this latter work, His gifts and works are greater, and His presence, even Himself, is greater than His works or gifts. His work in us prepares us for Himself. His gifts are the provisions of His presence. He places and makes us members of the body of Christ by His work. He keeps us in that body by His presence and person. He enables us to discharge our functions as members of that body by His gifts.

The whole lesson culminates in asking for the Holy Spirit as the great objective of all praying. In the direction in the Sermon on the Mount, we have the very plain and definite promise:

> *If you then, being evil, know how to give good gifts to your children, how much more will your Father who is in heaven give good things to those who ask him!*   (Matt. 7:11)

In Luke's version of this verse, *"good things"* is substituted by *"the Holy Spirit"* (Luke 11:13).

141

All good is comprehended in the Holy Spirit, and He is the sum and climax of all good things.

How complex, confusing, and involved are many human directions about obtaining the gift of the Holy Spirit as the abiding Comforter, our Sanctifier, and the One who empowers us! How simple and plain is our Lord's direction—Ask! Ask with urgency, ask without fainting. Ask, seek, knock, until He comes. Your heavenly Father will surely send Him if you ask for Him. Wait in the Lord for the Holy Spirit. It is the child waiting, asking, urging, and praying perseveringly for the Father's greatest gift and for the child's greatest need, the Holy Spirit.

The Holy Spirit Is for Those Who Ask

How are we to obtain the Holy Spirit so freely promised to those who seek Him believingly? Wait, press, and persevere with all the calmness and all the ardor of a faith that knows no fear, that allows no doubt, that does *"not waver at the promise of God through unbelief"* (Rom. 4:20), that in its darkest and most depressed hours believes in hope, that is brightened and strengthened by hope, and that is saved by hope.

Wait and pray: here are the keys that unlock every castle of despair and that open every treasure-house of God. This is the simplicity of the child's asking of the Father, who gives with a largeness, liberality, and cheerfulness infinitely above everything ever known to earthly parents.

Ask for the Holy Spirit; seek for the Holy Spirit; knock for the Holy Spirit. He is the Father's greatest gift for the child's greatest need.

In these three words, *"ask," "seek,"* and *"knock"* (Matt. 7:7), given to us by Christ, we have the repetition of the advancing steps of insistence and effort. He is laying Himself out in command and promise in the strongest way, showing us that if we will lay ourselves out in prayer and will persevere, rising to higher and stronger attitudes and sinking to deeper depths of intensity and effort, the answer must inevitably come. The stars would fail to shine before the asking, the seeking, and the knocking would fail to obtain what is needed and desired.

There is no elect company here, only the election of undismayed, importunate, never-fainting effort in prayer: *"To him who knocks it will be opened"* (Matt. 7:8; Luke 11:10). Nothing can be stronger than this declaration assuring us of the answer unless it is the promise on which it is based, *"So I say to you, ask, and it will be given to you"* (Luke 11:9).

And I will pray the Father, and He will give you another Helper, that He may abide with you forever.   —John 14:16

I will pray with the spirit, and I will also pray with the understanding.
                                    —1 Corinthians 14:15

Is anyone among you suffering? Let him pray. Is anyone cheerful? Let him sing psalms. Is anyone among you sick? Let him call for the elders of the church, and let them pray over him, anointing him with oil in the name of the Lord. And the prayer of faith will save the sick, and the Lord will raise him up. And if he has committed sins, he will be forgiven.   —James 5:13–15

Fourteen

The Holy Spirit, Our Helper in Prayer

We must pray in the Spirit, in the Holy Spirit, if we would pray at all. Lay this, I beseech you, to heart. Do not address yourselves to prayer as to a work to be accomplished in your own natural strength. It is a work of God, of God the Holy Spirit, a work of His in you and by you, and in which you must be fellow workers with Him—but His work notwithstanding.   —Archbishop Trench

One of the revelations of the New Testament concerning the Holy Spirit is that He is our Helper in prayer. So we see in the following incident in our Lord's life the close connection between the Holy Spirit's work and prayer:

In that hour Jesus rejoiced in the Spirit and said, "I thank You, Father, Lord of heaven and earth, that You have hidden these things from the wise and prudent and revealed them to babes. Even so, Father, for so it seemed good in Your sight." (Luke 10:21)

Prayer Connects the Father to the Child

In this passage we have revelations of what God is to us. Only the child's heart can know the Father, and only the child's heart can reveal the Father. It is only by prayer that all things are delivered to us by the Father through the Son. It is only by prayer that all things are revealed to us by the Father and by the Son. It is only in prayer that the Father gives Himself to us, which is much more in every way than all other things whatsoever.

The Holy Spirit Is Our Helper

The Revised Version reads, *"In that same hour he rejoiced in the Holy Spirit."* This sets forth that great truth not generally known, or if known, ignored, that Jesus Christ was generally led by the Holy Spirit, and that His joy and His praying, as well as His working and His life, were under the inspiration, law, and guidance of the Holy Spirit.

Turn to and read this passage: *"Likewise the Spirit also helps in our weaknesses. For we do not know what we should pray for as we ought"* (Rom. 8:26).

This text is most pregnant and vital, and needs to be quoted. Patience, hope, and waiting help us in prayer. But the greatest and the divinest of all helpers is the Holy Spirit. He takes hold of things for us. We are dark and confused, ignorant and weak in many things, in fact in everything pertaining to the heavenly life, especially in the simple service of prayer. There is an "ought" on us, an obligation, a necessity to pray, a spiritual necessity upon us of the most absolute and imperative kind. But we do not feel the obligation and have no ability to meet it. The Holy Spirit helps us in our weaknesses, gives wisdom to our ignorance, turns ignorance into wisdom, and changes our weakness into strength. The Spirit Himself does this. He helps and takes hold with us as we tug and toil. He adds His wisdom to our ignorance, gives His strength to our weakness. He pleads for us and in us. He quickens, illumines, and inspires our prayers. He composes and elevates the subject of our prayers and inspires the words and feelings of our prayers. He works mightily in us so that we can pray mightily. He enables us to pray always and ever according to the will of God.

Pray according to the Will of God

In 1 John 5 we have these words:

Now this is the confidence that we have in Him, that if we ask anything according to His will, He hears us. And if we know that He hears us, whatever we ask, we know that we have the petitions that we have asked of Him. (1 John 5:14–15)

What gives us boldness and so much freedom and fullness of approach toward God, the fact and basis of that boldness and liberty of approach, is that we are asking *"according to His will."* This does not mean submission, but conformity. *"According to"* means after the standard, conformity, agreement. We have boldness and all freedom of access to God because we are praying in conformity to His will. God records His general will in His Word, but He has this special work in praying for us to do.

How can we know the will of God in our praying? What are the things that God designs specially for us to do and pray? The Holy Spirit reveals them to us perpetually.

> *The Spirit Himself makes intercession for us with groanings which cannot be uttered. Now He who searches the hearts knows what the mind of the Spirit is, because He makes intercession for the saints according to the will of God.* (Rom. 8:26–27)

Combine this text with these words of Paul in First Corinthians:

> *But as it is written: "Eye has not seen, nor ear heard, nor have entered into the heart of man the things which God has prepared for those who love Him." But God has revealed them to us through His Spirit. For the Spirit searches all things, yes, the deep things of God. For what man knows the things of a man except the spirit of the man which is in him? Even so no one knows the things of God except the Spirit of God. Now we have received, not the spirit of the world, but the Spirit who is from God, that we might know*

the things that have been freely given to us by God. These things we also speak, not in words which man's wisdom teaches but which the Holy Spirit teaches, comparing spiritual things with spiritual. But the natural man does not receive the things of the Spirit of God, for they are foolishness to him; nor can he know them, because they are spiritually discerned. But he who is spiritual judges all things, yet he himself is rightly judged by no one. For "who has known the mind of the LORD that he may instruct Him?" But we have the mind of Christ.

(1 Cor. 2:9–16)

"Revealed them to us through His Spirit" (v. 10). Note these words. God searches the heart where the Spirit dwells and knows the mind of the Spirit. The Spirit who dwells in our hearts searches the deep purposes and the will of God for us, and reveals those purposes and that will of God, *"that we might know the things that have been freely given to us by God"* (v. 12). Our spirits are so fully indwelt by the Spirit of God, so responsive and obedient to His illumination and to His will, that we ask with holy boldness and freedom the things that the Spirit of God has shown us as the will of God, and faith is assured. Then *"we know that we have the petitions that we have asked of Him"* (1 John 5:15).

The Spirit Helps Us to Intercede

The natural man prays, but prays according to his own will, imagination, and desire. If he has

149

ardent desires and groanings, they are merely the fire and agony of nature, and not of the Spirit. What a world of natural praying there is, which is selfish, self-centered, self-inspired! The Spirit, when He prays through us, or helps us to meet the mighty "oughtness" of right praying, trims our praying down to the will of God, and then we give heart and expression to His unutterable groanings. Then *"we have the mind of Christ"* (1 Cor. 2:16), and pray as He would pray. His thoughts, purposes, and desires are our thoughts, purposes, and desires.

This revelation of the Spirit is not a new and different Bible from what we already have, but it is the Bible we have, applied personally by the Spirit. It is not new texts, but rather the Spirit's elevating of certain texts for us at the time.

It is the unfolding of the Word by the Spirit's light, guidance, and teaching, enabling us to perform the great office of intercessors on earth, in harmony with the great intercessions of Jesus Christ at the Father's right hand in heaven (Rom. 8:34).

We have in the Holy Spirit an illustration and an enabler of what this intercession is and ought to be. We are charged to supplicate in the Spirit and to pray in the Holy Spirit. We are reminded that the Holy Spirit *"helps in our weaknesses"* (v. 26), and that while intercession is an art of so divine and so high a nature that *"we do not know what we should pray for as we ought"* (v. 26), yet the Spirit teaches us this heavenly science, by making *"intercession for us with groanings which cannot be uttered"* (v. 26). How burdened are these intercessions of the Holy Spirit! How profoundly He feels the world's sin, the world's woe, and the world's loss, and how deeply He sympathizes with the dire conditions, are seen in His groanings that are too deep for utterance and too sacred to be voiced by Him. He inspires us to this most divine work of intercession, and His strength enables us to sigh unto God for the oppressed, the burdened, and the distressed creation. The Holy Spirit helps us in many ways.

How intense will be the intercessions of the saints who make their requests in the Spirit! How vain and delusive and how utterly fruitless and inefficient are prayers without the Spirit! Official prayers they may be, appropriate for state occasions, beautiful and courtly, but worth less than nothing as God values prayer.

Persevere in Prayer

It is our persevering prayers that will help the Holy Spirit to His mightiest work in us; and, at the same time, He helps us to these strenuous and exalted efforts in prayer.

We can and do pray by many inspirations and in many ways that are not of God. Many prayers are stereotyped in manner and in matter, in part, if not as a whole. Many prayers are hearty and vehement, but it is natural heartiness and a fleshly vehemence. Much praying is done out of habit and through form. Habit is a second nature and holds to the good, when so directed, as well as to the bad. The habit of praying is a good habit, and should be early and strongly formed, but to pray by habit alone is to destroy the life of prayer and allow it to degenerate into a hollow and false form. Habit may form the banks for the river of prayer, but there must be a strong, deep, pure current, crystal and life-giving, flowing between these two banks. Hannah multiplied her praying; she *"poured out* [her] *soul before the LORD"* (1 Sam. 1:15). We cannot make our prayer habits too marked and controlled if the life-waters are full and overflow the banks.

Pray in the Spirit

Our divine example in praying is the Son of God. Our divine Helper in praying is the Holy Spirit. He quickens us to pray and helps us in praying. Acceptable prayer must be begun and carried on by His presence and inspiration. We are charged in the Holy Scriptures to pray in the Holy Spirit: *"Praying always with all prayer and supplication in the Spirit"* (Eph. 6:18). We are also encouraged with these words:

> *Likewise the Spirit also helps in our weaknesses. For we do not know what we should pray for as we ought, but the Spirit Himself makes intercession for us with groanings which cannot be uttered. Now He who searches the hearts knows what the mind of the Spirit is, because He makes intercession for the saints according to the will of God.*
> (Rom. 8:26–27)

So ignorant are we in this matter of prayer, so impotent are all other teachers to impart its lessons to our understanding and heart, that the Holy Spirit comes as the infallible and all-wise Teacher to instruct us in this divine art. As someone has said, "To pray with all your heart and all your strength, with the reason and the will, this is the greatest achievement of the Christian warfare on earth." This is what we are taught to do and enabled to do by the Holy Spirit. If no man can say that Jesus is the Christ except by the Spirit's help (1 Cor. 12:3), for a much greater reason, no man can pray except with the help of God's Spirit. Our mother's lips, perhaps now sealed by death, taught us many sweet lessons of prayer—prayers that have bound and held our hearts like golden threads; but these prayers, flowing through the natural channel of a mother's love, cannot serve the challenges and storms of our adult life. These maternal lessons are but the ABCs of praying. For the higher and graduate lessons in prayer, we must have the Holy Spirit. He only can unfold to us the mysteries of the prayer life, its duty and its service.

The Holy Spirit Abides within Us

To pray by the Holy Spirit we must have Him, always. He does not, like earthly teachers, teach us the lesson and then withdraw. He stays to help us practice the lessons He has taught. We do not pray by the precepts and lessons He has taught, but we pray by Him. He is both Teacher and Lesson.

We can know the lesson only because He is ever with us, to inspire, to illumine, to explain, to help us to do. We do not pray by the truth the Holy Spirit reveals to us, but we pray by the actual presence of the Holy Spirit. He puts the desire in our hearts and kindles that desire by His own flame. We simply give lip and voice and heart to His unutterable groanings. Our prayers are taken up by Him and energized and sanctified by His intercession. He prays for us, through us, and in us. We pray by Him, through Him, and in Him. He puts the prayer in us, and we give it utterance and heart.

We always pray *"according to the will of God"* (Rom. 8:27) when the Holy Spirit helps our praying. He prays through us only *"according to the will of God."* If our prayers are not *"according to the will of God,"* they die in the presence of the Holy Spirit. He gives such prayers no approval, no help. Disclaimed and unhelped by Him, prayers that are not according to God's will soon die out of every heart where the Holy Spirit dwells.

We must, as Jude said, "[Pray] *in the Holy Spirit"* (Jude 20). As Paul said, we should always pray *"with all prayer and supplication in the Spirit"* (Eph. 6:18). Never forget that

> *the Spirit also helps in our weaknesses. For we do not know what we should pray for as we ought, but the Spirit Himself makes intercession for us with groanings which cannot be uttered.* (Rom. 8:26)

Above all, over all, and through all, our praying must be in the name of Christ, which includes the power of His blood, the energy of His intercession, and the fullness of His royal authority. *"Whatever you ask in My name, that I will do"* (John 14:13).

And whenever you stand praying, if you have anything against anyone, forgive him, that your Father in heaven may also forgive you your trespasses.

—Mark 11:25

But you, beloved, building yourselves up on your most holy faith, praying in the Holy Spirit, keep yourselves in the love of God, looking for the mercy of our Lord Jesus Christ unto eternal life.

—Jude 20–21

Give ear, O LORD, to my prayer; and attend to the voice of my supplications.

—Psalm 86:6

Fifteen

The Two Comforters and Two Advocates

If we were asked whose Comforter the Holy Spirit was, the answer would be: Ours. The answer is not so ready when we are asked whose Advocate He is. The Spirit is Christ's Advocate, not ours. It is Christ's place He takes, Christ's cause He pleads, Christ's name He vindicates, Christ's kingdom He administers. —Samuel Chadwick

T he fact that man has two divine Comforters, Advocates, and Helpers declares the affluence of God's provisions in the Gospel, and also the settled purpose of God to execute His work of salvation with efficacy and final success. Many-sided are the infirmities and needs of man in his pilgrimage and warfare for heaven. These two Christs—Jesus and the Holy Spirit—can join together with manifold wisdom.

God's Resources Are Boundless

The affluence of God's provision of two Intercessors in executing the plan of salvation finds its counterpart in the following prayer promise in its unlimited nature, encompassing all things, great and small. *"Whatever things you ask in prayer, believing, you will receive"* (Matt. 21:22). We have all things in Christ, all things in the Holy Spirit, and all things in prayer.

The Two Christs

How much is ours in God's plan and purposes in these two Christs, the One ascended to heaven and enthroned there to intercede for our benefit, the Other, His Representative, and better Substitute (see John 14:12), on earth, to work in us and make intercessions for us!

The first Christ was a person who came in human flesh (John 1:14). The other Christ is a person, but not clothed in physical form or subject to human limitations as the first Christ necessarily was. Transient and local was the first Christ. The other Christ is not limited to locality; not transient, but abiding. He does not deal with the material, the fleshly, but enters personally into the mysterious and imperial domain of the spirit, to emancipate and transform into more than Eden-beauty that desolate and dark realm. The first Christ left His novitiates that they might enter into higher regions of spiritual knowledge. The man-Christ withdrew so that the Spirit-Christ might train and school into the deeper mysteries of God, so that all the historical and physical might be transmuted into the pure gold of the spiritual. The first Christ brought to us a picture of what we must be. The other Christ mirrored this perfect and fadeless image on our hearts. The first Christ, like David, gathered and furnished the material for the temple. The other Christ forms God's glorious temple out of this material.

The Two Intercessors

The possibilities of prayer, then, are the possibilities of these two divine Intercessors. Where are the limitations to results when the Holy Spirit intercedes *"for us with groanings which cannot be uttered"* (Rom. 8:26), when He so helps us that our prayers run parallel to the will of God, and we pray for the very things and in the very manner in which we ought to pray, schooled in and pressed to these prayers by the urgency of the Holy Spirit! How measureless are the possibilities of prayer when we are *"filled with all the fullness of God"* (Eph. 3:19), when we *"stand perfect and complete in all the will of God"* (Col. 4:12)!

If the intercession of Moses so wondrously preserved the being and safety of Israel throughout its marvelous history and destiny, what may we not secure through our Intercessor, who is so much greater than Moses? All that God has lies open to Christ through prayer. All that Christ has lies open to us through prayer.

The Holy Spirit Makes Christ Known

If we have the two Christs covering the whole realm of goodness, power, purity, and glory, in heaven and on earth—if we have the better Christ with us here in this world—why is it that we sigh to know the Christ in the flesh as the disciples knew Him? (See 2 Corinthians 5:16.) Why is it that the mighty work of these two almighty Intercessors finds us so barren of heavenly fruit, so feeble in all Christlike principles, so low in the Christlike life, and so marred in the Christlike image? Is it not because our prayers for the Holy Spirit have been so faint and few? The heavenly Christ can come to us in full beauty and power only when we have received the fullness of the present earthly Christ, even the Holy Spirit.

Living always the life of prayer, breathing always the spirit of prayer, being always in the fact of prayer, *"praying always...in the Spirit"* (Eph. 6:18), the heavenly Christ would become ours by a clearer vision, a deeper love, and a more intimate fellowship than He was to His disciples in the days of His flesh.

We would not disguise or lessen the fact that there is a loss to us by our absent Christ as we will see and know Him in heaven. But in our earthly work to be done by us, and above all to be done in us, we will know Christ and the Father better, and can better utilize them by the ministry of the Holy Spirit than would have been possible under the personal, human presence of the Son. So to the loving and obedient one who is filled with the Spirit, both the Father and the Son *"will come to him and make* [Their] *home with him"* (John 14:23). In the day of the fullness of the indwelling

Spirit, *"You will know that I am in My Father, and you in Me, and I in you"* (John 14:20). Amazing oneness and harmony, wrought by the almighty power of the other Christ!

The Holy Spirit Brings the Fullness of God

There is not a note in the archangel's song with which the Holy Spirit does not attune man into sympathy, not a pulsation in the heart of God to which the Holy Spirit-filled heart does not respond with loud amens and joyful hallelujahs. Even more than this, by the other Christ, the Holy Spirit, we *"know the love of Christ which passes knowledge"* (Eph. 3:19). More than this, by the Holy Spirit we are *"filled with all the fullness of God"* (v. 19). More than this, God *"is able to do exceedingly abundantly above all that we ask or think, according to the power that works in us"* (v. 20).

The presence and power of the other Christ more than compensated the disciples for the loss of the first Christ. His going away had filled their hearts with a strange sorrow. A loneliness and desolation like an orphan's woe had swept over their hearts and stunned and bewildered them; but He comforted them by telling them that the coming of the Holy Spirit would be like the rapture of a travailing mother who has just given birth—all the pain is forgotten in the untold joy that a man-child has been born into the world.

The LORD is far from the wicked, but He hears the prayer of the righteous.

—Proverbs 15:29

Assuredly, I say to you, if you have faith and do not doubt, you will not only do what was done to the fig tree, but also if you say to this mountain, "Be removed and be cast into the sea," it will be done. And whatever things you ask in prayer, believing, you will receive.

—Matthew 21:21–22

We will give ourselves continually to prayer and to the ministry of the word.

—Acts 6:4

Sixteen

Prayer and the Holy Spirit Dispensation

How God needs, how the world needs, how the church needs the flow of the mighty river more blessed than the Nile, deeper, broader, and more overflowing than the Amazon's mighty current! And yet what mere little brooks we are! We need, the age needs, the church needs memorials of God's mighty power, which will silence the Enemy and the Avenger, dumbfound God's foes, strengthen weak saints, and fill strong ones with triumphant raptures.   —E. M. Bounds

The dispensation of the Holy Spirit was ushered in by prayer. Read these words from Acts:

When they had entered, they went up into the upper room where they were staying: Peter, James, John, and Andrew; Philip and Thomas; Bartholomew and Matthew; James the son of Alphaeus and Simon the Zealot; and Judas the son of James. These all continued with one accord in prayer and supplication,

with the women and Mary the mother of Je-
sus, and with His brothers. (Acts 1:13–14)

This oneness of accord in prayer was the attitude that the disciples assumed after Jesus had
ascended to heaven. Their meeting for prayer ushered in the dispensation of the Holy Spirit, to
which prophets had looked forward with en-
tranced vision. And to prayer, in a marked way,
has this dispensation, which holds in its keeping
the fortune of the Gospel, been committed.

Put Prayer First

Apostolic men knew well the worth of prayer
and were jealous of the most sacred offices that
infringed on their time and strength and hindered
them from giving themselves *"continually to
prayer and to the ministry of the word"* (Acts 6:4).
They put prayer first. The Word depends on
prayer so that it *"may run swiftly and be glorified"*
(2 Thess. 3:1). Praying apostles make preaching
apostles. Prayer gives edge, entrance, and weight
to the Word. Sermons conceived by prayer and
saturated with prayer are weighty sermons. Sermons may be ponderous with thought, sparkle
with the gems of genius and of taste, pleasing and
popular, but unless they have their birth and life
in prayer, for God's uses, they are of little value,
dull and dead.

The Lord of the harvest sends out laborers,
full in number and perfect in kind, in answer to

prayer. (See Matthew 9:38.) No prophetic vision is needed to declare that if the church had used prayer force to its utmost, the light of the Gospel would have long since encircled the world.

God's Gospel has always waited more on prayer than on anything else for its successes. A praying church is strong, though poor in all besides. A prayerless church is weak, though rich in all besides. Only praying hearts will build God's kingdom. Only praying hands will put the crown on the Savior's head.

Be Filled with the Spirit

The Holy Spirit is the divinely appointed Substitute for and Representative of the personal and humanized Christ. How much He is to us! And how we are to be filled by Him, live in Him, walk in Him, and be led by Him! How we are to conserve and kindle to a brighter and more consuming glow the holy flame! How careful should we be never to quench that pure flame! How watchful, tender, and loving ought we to be so as not to grieve His sensitive, loving nature! How attentive, meek, and obedient we should be, never resisting His divine impulses, always listening for His voice, and always ready to do His divine will. How can all this be done without much and continuous prayer?

The importunate widow had a great case to win against helpless, hopeless despair, but she did it by persevering prayer. (See Luke 18: 1–8.) We have this great treasure to preserve and enhance, but we have a divine Person who will maintain and help us. We can be enabled to meet our duties only by much prayer.

Prayer is the only element in which the Holy Spirit can live and work. Prayer is the golden chain that happily enslaves Him to His happy work in us.

Everything depends upon our having this Second Christ and retaining Him in the fullness of His power. With the disciples, Pentecost was made by prayer. With them, Pentecost was continued by their giving themselves to continued prayer. Persistent and unwearied prayer is the price we will have to pay for our Pentecost, by immediate and continued prayer. Abiding in the fact and in the spirit of prayer is the only surety of our abiding in Pentecostal power and purity.

The Holy Spirit Enlarges Our Prayer

Not only should the many-sided operation of the Holy Spirit in us and for us teach us the necessity of prayer for Him, but also His condition with our praying assumes another attitude, the attitude of mutual dependence, that of action and reaction. The more we pray, the more He helps us to pray, and the larger the measure of Himself He gives to us. We are not only to pray and press and wait for His coming to us, but after we have received Him in His fullness, we are also to pray for a fuller and still larger bestowment of Himself to us. We are to pray for the largest, ever increasing, and constant fullness of capacity. Paul prayed this prayer for the Spirit-baptized Ephesian church:

That He would grant you, according to the riches of His glory, to be strengthened with might through His Spirit in the inner man, that Christ may dwell in your hearts through faith; that you, being rooted and grounded in love, may be able to comprehend with all the saints what is the width and length and depth and height; to know the love of Christ which passes knowledge; that you may be filled with all the fullness of God. (Eph. 3:16–19)

In that wonderful prayer for those Christians, Paul laid himself out to pray to God, and by prayer he sought to fathom the fathomless depths and to measure the measureless purposes and benefits of God's plan of salvation for immortal souls by the presence and work of the Holy Spirit. Only importunate and invincible prayer can bring the Holy Spirit to us and secure for us these indescribable, gracious results. *"Always laboring fervently for you in prayers, that you may stand perfect and complete in all the will of God"* (Col. 4:12).

The Holy Spirit Brings Power

The Word of God provides for a mighty, consciously realized faith in His saints, into whose happy, shining spirits God has been brought as a Dweller, and whose heaven-toned lives have been attuned to God's melody by His own hand.

Then will it prove true: *"He who believes in Me, as the Scripture has said, out of his heart will flow rivers of living water"* (John 7:38). This Scripture is a promise concerning the indwelling and outflowing of the Holy Spirit in us—life-giving, fruitful, irresistible, a ceaseless outflow of the river of God in us.

How God needs, how the world needs, how the church needs the flow of this mighty river; again, it is more blessed than the Nile, deeper, broader, and more overflowing than the Amazon's broad and mighty current! And yet what mere little brooks we are and have!

Oh, that the church, by the infilling and out-flowing of Holy Spirit, might be able to raise up everywhere memorials of the Holy Spirit's power, which might fix the eye as well as engage the heart! We need, the age needs, the church needs, memorials of God's mighty power, which will silence the Enemy and the Avenger, dumbfound God's foes, strengthen weak saints, and fill strong ones with triumphant raptures.

The Holy Spirit Brings Assurance of Salvation

A glance at more of the divine promises concerning this vital question of the Holy Spirit working in us would show us how these promises need to be projected into the experiential and the actual. Jesus said, *"If anyone wants do His will, he shall know concerning the doctrine, whether it is from God or whether I speak on My own authority"* (John 7:17). How we need a conscious faith, personal and vital, unspeakable in its joy, and full of glory (1 Pet. 1:8)! The need is for a conscious faith, made so by the Spirit bearing *"witness with our spirit that we are children of God"* (Rom. 8:16). A faith of "I know" is the only powerful, vital, and aggressive religion. *"One thing I know: that though I was blind, now I see"* (John 9:25). We need men and women in these loose days who can verify the above-mentioned promise of Christ in their inner consciousnesses. And yet how many untold thousands of people in all of our churches have only a dim, impalpable, "I hope so, maybe so, I trust so," kind of religion, all dubious, intangible, and unstable.

In these days, there is certainly a great need in the church, first, for Christians to see and seek and obtain the high privilege in the Gospel of a heaven-born, clear-cut, and happy religious experience, born of the presence of the Holy Spirit, giving an undoubted assurance of sins forgiven, and of adoption into the family of God.

The Holy Spirit Brings Purity and Power

Second, there is a need in believers' lives, subsequent to this conscious realization of divine favor in the forgiveness of sins, and added to it, for the reception of the Holy Spirit in His fullness. He will purify their hearts by faith, perfecting them in love, helping them to overcome the world; bestow a divine, inward power over all sin, both inward and outward; give boldness to bear witness; and qualify them for real service in the church and in the world.

There is a fearfully prevailing agnosticism in the church at this time. I greatly fear that a vast majority of our church members are now in this school of spiritual agnosticism, and really deem it to be a virtue to be there. God's Word gives no encouragement whatever to a shadowy religion and a vague religious experience. It calls us definitely into the realm of knowledge. It crowns religion with the crown of "I know." It passes us from the darkness of sin, doubt, and inward misgivings into the marvelous light, where we see clearly and know fully our personal relationship to God.

> The things unknown to feeble sense,
> Unseen by reason's glimmering ray,
> With strong, commanding confidence,
> Their heavenly origin display.

Two things may be said in conclusion: First, this sort of Bible religion comes directly through the office of the Holy Spirit dealing personally with each soul; second, the Holy Spirit in all of His offices pertaining to spiritual life and religious experience is secured by earnest, definite, prevailing prayer.

ANOTHER POWERFUL *B*OOK
from Whitaker House

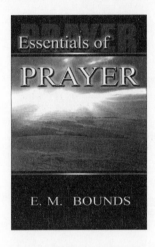

Essentials of Prayer
E. M. Bounds

If praying has become a task, something healthy that you keep putting off, it may be that you're missing a critical truth that could break you into a place of intimacy and power. E. M. Bounds will challenge you and teach you how to sustain a practice of power-packed, life-changing prayer. Do more than dream about an effective prayer life!

ISBN: 0-88368-708-9 • Trade • 144 pages

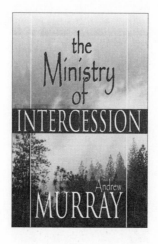

ANOTHER POWERFUL *Book*
from Whitaker House

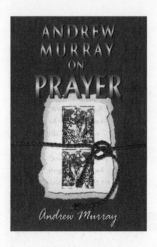

Andrew Murray on Prayer
Andrew Murray

Combining seven of Andrew Murray's most well-known works on prayer, this book will give you biblical guidelines for effective, vital communication with God. Discover the essential keys to developing a vital prayer life, and begin to reap the benefits of true prayer.

ISBN: 0-88368-528-0   Trade   656 pages

ANOTHER POWERFUL BOOK

from Whitaker House

Spurgeon on Prayer and Spiritual Warfare
Charles H. Spurgeon

Many keys to living a successful Christian life can be found in these practical words by Charles Spurgeon—keys to praying, praising, and warring against Satan. Victory in Christ can be yours as you implement these vital truths. Answered prayers and a deeper faith in God await you.

ISBN: 0-88368-527-2   Trade   576 pages

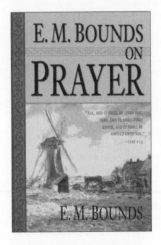